JERUSALEM TESTAMENT

JERUSALEM TESTAMENT

Palestinian Christians Speak, 1988-2008

Melanie A. May

William B. Eerdmans Publishing Company
Grand Rapids, Michigan / Cambridge, U.K.

Published 2010 by

Wm. B. Eerdmans Publishing Co.

2140 Oak Industrial Drive N.E., Grand Rapids, Michigan 49505 /

P.O. Box 163, Cambridge CB3 9PU U.K.

Printed in the United States of America

14 13 12 11 10   7 6 5 4 3 2 1

Library of Congress Cataloging-in-Publication Data

May, Melanie A.

    Jerusalem testament: Palestinian Christians speak, 1988-2008 / Melanie May.

       p.   cm.

    ISBN 978-0-8028-6485-7 (pbk.: alk. paper)

    1. Christians — Jerusalem.   2. Palestinian Arabs — Jerusalem — Religion.

    3. Christians — Jerusalem — Social conditions.

    4. Palestinian Arabs — Jerusalem — Social conditions.   I. Title.

BR1113.J5M38   2010

956.9405′408827 — dc22

                                    2009042575

www.eerdmans.com

For Xavier and Matthias, Tate and Ross,
who light a spark in Mayma's eyes,
as did their dear Nana.

For the children of the land called holy
— Christian, Jew, Muslim, Druse —
that peace and justice may light a spark
in the eyes of them all.

Contents

Acknowledgments

Every text is intertextual. *Jerusalem Testament* is no exception. First and foremost, *Jerusalem Testament* is a testament of the Jerusalem Heads of Churches, who issued joint public statements from January 1988 through January 2008. They have continued to issue statements as pastors and as spiritual representatives of faithful — often forgotten — Christians of the Holy Land. I continue to be deeply moved by the courage and the steadfast hope to which the Heads of Jerusalem Churches bear witness.

Without the urging of Dr. Anna Marie Aagaard, Professor Emerita of the University of Aarhus and immediate past president of the World Council of Churches, I would not have pursued this research and writing project. Aware that a long-overdue sabbatical leave was on my horizon and knowing about my years of study and travel in the Holy Land, as well as my ecumenical experience, she said to me, "This is the project for your sabbatical." I am deeply grateful for Anna Marie's sage advice and for the gift of her friendship.

I could not have accomplished this research and writing project without the wise counsel of Fr. Frans Bouwen, White Father, Fr. Thomas Stransky, C.S.P. Frans, an ecumenist in Jerusalem and with the World Council of Churches' Commission on Faith and Order, and longtime resident at St. Anne's in the Old City, and Tom, an ecumenist formed on the front lines at the Second Vatican Council and former Rector of Tantur; they have been constant companions and conversation partners. They have unfailingly given insight into the complexities and confounding nuances that characterize the traditions and present realities of church life in the Holy City. I am also honored by the generous hospitality extended to me by the community of St. Anne's: at table, in the refectory, in the library, and at the photocopier.

The generous hospitality extended by Tantur Ecumenical Institute is woven into each word of *Jerusalem Testament.* Every member of the staff — at the reception desk, in the kitchen and refectory, in the library and laundry, and on the grounds — has been amazingly welcoming. I give very especial thanks to God for Fr. Michael McGarry, C.S.P., Rector of Tantur Ecumenical Institute, and to Sr. Bridget Tighe, F.M.D.M., Vice Rector. Michael and Bridget welcomed me for four months during the fall term of 2007, and again for a month in May-June of 2008 and a month in May-June of 2009. The fruits of table fellowship, conversation over coffee in the Bethlehem Room, and various excursions with Michael and with Bridget have all been of inestimable aid at every stage in this research and writing project. Tantur has truly been a home-away-from-home. I am indeed grateful.

Jean Zaru offered some of the most memorable hours of friendship and fellowship in her lovely home in Ramallah. Her Palestinian cooking is without peer. And her tell-it-like-it-is wisdom, fired in the crucible of life as a Palestinian living on the West Bank since the 1940s, was and is ever my reality check. Her ever-ready and rapier wit is my delight, and our laughter together a balm for my spirit.

I am also deeply grateful for the sustaining support of my home institution, Colgate Rochester Crozer Divinity School, in Rochester, New York, whose ambassador I am proud to be. My thanks in particular to the Board of Trustees for the gift of sabbatical time, to President Eugene C. Bay and my cherished faculty colleagues, and to the staff whose presence made my absence possible.

When it comes to publishing plans, no one else's advice and counsel comes close to that of my dear friend Rev. Norman J. Hjelm. I yet again give thanks to God for the gift of his friendship through many years as our paths have brought us together in a variety of venues and during defining times of our lives. I continue to learn so much from Norman, and I take heart from his steadfast faith in all of life's seasons.

I give thanks for more friends than I can name; they have breathed life into my spirit while this project was in process, and continue to do so. My heart is full. My highest joy is family: my beloved stepchildren (and friends!) and grandchildren: Megan and Catherine, Xavier and Matthias; Karen Colin, Tate, and Ross; my dear siblings and in-laws, nieces and nephews: Greg, Anna, and Julia; Jonathan, Allison, Jessica, Brian, and Benjamin; Lisa, Chris, Nathan, Thomas, and Andrew. Thanks be to God, indeed!

Introduction

On 22 January 1988, the Jerusalem Heads of Churches issued the first of what would, by 22 January, 2008, be sixty-eight joint public statements on the situation of Palestinian Christians in the Holy Land, and especially in the Holy City, Jerusalem. These twenty years began with the outbreak of the first Intifada and ended with the siege of Gaza. Life amid such relentless conflict often rends communities asunder. These statements of common witness by the Heads of Christian Communities in Jerusalem are, therefore, all the more remarkable. Living under Israeli occupation — suffering deprivation, harassment, restriction of movement, surveillance[1] — Christians in Jerusalem, for the first time in centuries, bear a common witness to their faith and to their hope: an end to occupation and a just peace.[2]

Accordingly, these statements by the Jerusalem Heads of Churches are addressed to "our people." Statements were read aloud in worship services and posted in church halls. But the Jerusalem Heads of Churches also spoke as representatives of "our people," and addressed presidents and prime ministers, and also appealed to the worldwide Christian and international communities: "We, the Heads of the Christian Communities in the Holy City, have met together in view of the grave situation prevailing in Jerusalem and the whole of our country. It is our Christian conviction that as Spiritual Leaders we have an urgent duty to follow up the developments of this situation and to make known to the world the conditions of life of our people here in the Holy Land."[3] The act of issuing these statements was, therefore, both a pastoral and a political act.[4]

In this volume, statements issued by the Jerusalem Heads of Churches, 1988-2008, are, for the first time, collected together and presented as a body of texts. Work on this body of texts began during the fall of 2007 when I was a Scholar at Tantur Ecumenical Institute, Jerusalem, on the road to Bethlehem. While there I planned to track down these statements in order to introduce Palestinian Christian voices more fully into Western Christian discussions of the seemingly intractable Israeli-Palestinian conflict. In advance, my mentors and friends, Professor Anna Marie Aagaard, University of Aarhus, Denmark, and Father Frans Bouwen, a Belgian Benedictine White Father who has lived at St. Anne's, Jerusalem, since 1969, thought I might find thirty-five to forty such statements. And I had imagined I would begin by finding a perhaps disheveled, but nonetheless extant, file in an ecclesial archive in Jerusalem. As soon as I arrived in Jerusalem, however, I was advised that life under occupation did not afford the luxury of creating or maintaining archives. I therefore spent weeks searching through monthly bulletins and quarterly journals in various libraries and information centers in Jerusalem. I found complete texts; I also followed oblique references. Slowly, the list of statements lengthened, and the contours and content of this "Jerusalem Testament" emerged.

I have named this body of texts "Jerusalem Testament" because first and foremost these statements by the Jerusalem Heads of Churches bear witness. They bear witness to the Gospel of Jesus Christ as they bear witness to the faith and hope of Palestinian Christians, "our people." More particularly, the statements bear witness to the faith and hope of particular Christians living in a particular place, Jerusalem, who keep alive the faith of Jesus as heirs of the earliest church. The statements proclaim the faith of the church anew, incarnate in the lives of Christians living in the land of Jesus' birth, death, resurrection, and ascension.

This body of texts is also a testament because it calls to all Christians in all places: "If the child cannot be born in our hearts, then the child will not be born at all. Are we willing to transform our hearts into cribs that are ready to receive God and facilitate his presence within us?"[5] This testament thereby calls Christians worldwide to a new covenant with sisters and brothers in the Holy City, Jerusalem, who live under the more and more dangerously deteriorated conditions of Israeli occupation and dispossession.

As I write this introduction in mid-June 2008, the urgency undulating through this testament is palpably present. I sit in the front garden at Tantur, shaded by cedar trees, surrounded by flowering geraniums and roses, rosemary and lavender. Trees hang heavy with their fruits. I am lulled by the lilting songs of birds. But if I look beyond this garden to next-door Bethlehem, my view is blocked by the ubiquitous Wall.[6] And just minutes ago Tantur staff brought news that demolition orders have been issued for twelve Palestinian houses just west of Bethlehem, a few miles from the paradisal place I sit. It seems that, after a hiatus, house demolitions may begin again.[7] And in recent days Palestinian friends spoke of the ever-worsening situation: Jerusalemite Christians leaving in ever-greater numbers;[8] Jerusalemite identity cards becoming harder and harder to maintain;[9] the unimaginably severe humanitarian crisis in besieged Gaza;[10] visas more difficult to obtain for international clergy and church workers; an increased number of checkpoints on the West Bank; new housing units to be built in East Jerusalem settlements[11] and in the Har Homa settlement that sits on the hill across from Tantur. The occupation in its awful flesh-and-blood reality — IDF-manned checkpoints and barricades; helicopter gunships; targeted assassinations; military incursions in the middle of the night; massive theft of Palestinian land — invades every inch of Palestinian daily life.

And the displacement and dispossession of Palestinians which began in 1948 — the Nakba[12] — is now in its 62nd year. On 14 May 2008, Israelis celebrated the 60th anniversary of the declaration of the State of Israel. On that day Palestinians remembered the massacre of Deir Yassin,[13] a village near Jerusalem in which women, children, and old men were struck down in cold blood. They remembered that when news of this massacre — "Deir Yassin, Deir Yassin" — spread across villages and howled through olive groves, thousands of families fled to escape a similar fate. They remembered the forced and re-enforced exile of 750,000 Palestinians: refugees still being refused the right to return to their villages and homes, to their lands and olive groves. Palestinians remembered the squalor of refugee camps, many of which are still populated by a fourth generation, as the temporary has lengthened into timeless limbo. The catastrophe continues: in the camps; in blockaded Gaza; in the open-air prison that is the West Bank.[14]

Palestinian remembrance and reality pulse — an urgent ululation — through the statements of the Jerusalem Heads of Churches. Palestinian remembrance and reality urgently impel the publication of this "Jerusalem Testament."

The Jerusalem Churches, the Heads of which issued these statements, are diverse. The histories of these churches are centuries long and tangled.

The Christological controversies of the fourth and fifth centuries divided major Christian communities and planted seeds of distrust. But, as has been suggested above, the sharp rupture between churches of the Greek and Latin rites was neither clear nor confirmed until the arrival of the Crusaders in 1099. Even during the century thereafter it seems these Latin Christians worked together with the indigenous Christians to repair ruined Holy Places, and Christians with differing languages and rites worshiped in the Holy Sepulchre. A series of events slowly but surely shifted this situation of co-existence: the conquest of Jerusalem by Salah ad-Din in 1187; the sacking of Constantinople by Frankish Crusaders in 1204; and the fall of Constantinople to Sultan Mohammed II in 1453, which confirmed with finality the 1054 schism between Eastern and Western Christendom. Indeed, Byzantine Christians soon discovered they preferred the tolerance with which the Muslim sultan treated his subject peoples over the previous three hundred years of heavy-handed Latin, albeit Christian, rule.

Disputes over possession and the right of pre-eminence in the Holy Places rose to bitter heights in the sixteenth century with the establishment of the Ottoman Empire in Palestine in 1517. During the four centuries of Ottoman rule, the history of the churches of Jerusalem is a history of this conflict — conflict that most embroiled the Greek Orthodox Church and the Custodia Terrae Sanctae, established in 1217 as a special branch of the Franciscan order to defend and protect the Holy Places that were in Muslim hands. For centuries the Custodia filled the gap left when the Latin Patriarch fled following Salah ad-Din's capture of the city in 1187.[15] Here, as I briefly introduce these churches, I hope to underscore how remarkable it is that, given the centuries of conflicted history, the Jerusalem Heads of Churches could — amid another bitterly conflicted history — together bear common witness to faith and to hope. I thereby attempt to prepare readers to more fully understand the significance of the joint, public statements made by the Jerusalem Heads of Churches.[16]

The Greek Orthodox Church is the largest of the churches, and lays claim to the Apostle James, brother of Jesus, first bishop of Jerusalem, as founder. But Jerusalem was not one of the ancient sees[17] until the Council of Chalcedon raised the rank of Bishop of Jerusalem to Patriarch of Jerusalem in 451 C.E. Since that time, except during the years of the Latin Crusader Kingdom when the Patriarch fled for safety to Constantinople, the resident Patriarch of Jerusalem of the Greek Orthodox Church has held the status of first among the Jerusalem Heads of Churches. As waves of pilgrimage swelled, and with the support of tsarist Russia from the late eighteenth century, the Greek Orthodox Church acquired considerable assets.[18]

Other Orthodox churches are the Armenian Orthodox, the Coptic Orthodox, the Ethiopian Orthodox, and the Syrian Orthodox Churches. These four churches are defined by their non-acceptance of the decision of the Council of Chalcedon on Christological issues. Specifically, these churches did not, and do not, accept the Chalcedonian Christological formula "two natures in one Person." Instead, following the fourth-century Cyril of Alexandria, they confess there is one incarnate nature of God the Logos. The unified person Jesus Christ cannot be separated into divine and human components. For many centuries, these churches were, therefore, called "monophysite churches." Now they identify themselves as Oriental Orthodox Churches, while the churches in the East who accepted the outcome of the Council of Chalcedon are called the Eastern Orthodox Churches.[19]

Among the Oriental Orthodox Churches, the Head of the Armenian Orthodox Church is one of the three Patriarchs who are guardians of the Holy Places. There is archaeological evidence of the presence of the Armenian Church from the beginnings of the Christian Era. Armenian monks lived with Greek monks in monasteries and deserts in and around Jerusalem. Already in 301 C.E., Armenia had adopted Christianity as the official state religion — the first nation to do so. Thereafter, Armenian Christians went on pilgrimage to Jerusalem. Soon what is known as the Armenian Quarter, located in the Old City's southeast corner, was established. In the fourth century, St. James' Cathedral was built on the site where the present cathedral stands. In the seventh century, when Arab Muslims came into the Holy Land, there is documentary evidence of the Armenian Bishops of Jerusalem.

The third Patriarch of Jerusalem, together with the Greek and Armenian, is the Latin Patriarch. Roman Catholics have been known as the Latins since the time of the Crusades and the twelfth-century Crusader kingdom, beginning 1099 C.E. When, as was noted above, the Latin Crusader kingdom was defeated by Salah ad-Din in the twelfth century, the Latin Patriarch fled the city. A titular Latin Patriarchate existed in exile until it once again became a residency in Jerusalem in 1847 C.E.

The re-establishment of a resident Latin Patriarch opened the way for the establishment of schools and for the arrival of numerous religious orders. As noted above, the Franciscan Fathers[20] had already established the Custodia Terrae Sanctae in the Holy Land, and in 1342 the Custodia received papal recognition of rights to the Holy Places, rights which had already been obtained in 1333 from the sultan by Robert of Anjou, king of Naples. The Custodia Terrae Sanctae is headed by the Custos, a Franciscan priest.[21] The Custos, and the three Patriarchs of Jerusalem, are the foremost signatories to the statements of the Jerusalem Heads of Churches.

The Jerusalem Heads of other Catholic Churches have also signed the statements: the Patriarchal Vicar of the Maronite Church of Antioch, which is the largest church in Lebanon (where it was founded); and the Patriarchal Vicars of the Syrian Catholic Church and the Armenian Catholic Church. These two churches emerged in the mid-eighteenth century out of "a clear-cut definitive rupture" between Catholic and Orthodox hierarchies in the Middle East.[22] The churches are still marked by the rupture: while their liturgies are redolent of Orthodox liturgy, both are in communion with Rome.

The largest member of the Catholic Church family is the Greek Catholic (Melkite) Church, founded in 1724 after a split with the Greek Orthodox Patriarch of Antioch. It is, after the Greek Orthodox Church, the largest church in the Holy Land, having a particularly strong presence along the northern coast, from Acre to Haifa, and in the Galilee. In 1838, the Greek Catholic Patriarch was finally recognized by the sultan; about the same time, the pope conferred the additional titles of Alexandria and of Jerusalem, leading to the residency of the Greek Catholic Patriarchal Vicar in Jerusalem.

Signatories of the statements of the Jerusalem Heads of Churches include two Protestants: the Bishop of the Episcopal Church of Jerusalem and the Middle East, and the Bishop of the Evangelical Lutheran Church in Jordan and the Holy Land. Protestant churches only occasionally appeared in Jerusalem until the early decades of the nineteenth century. However, Protestant missionaries were at a distinct disadvantage, having neither legal status in the Ottoman Empire nor the support of a European power. In the mid-1830s, just after the occupation of Jerusalem by the Egyptian pasha, Muhammad Ali, in 1834, an appeal was sent to England "to start a 'Hebrew Church and Mission in Jerusalem.'"[23] In 1836, the liturgy of the Church of England was translated into Hebrew; two years later, a plot of land was purchased just inside the Jaffa Gate, across from the Citadel of

David. In 1841, the Prussian King Frederick William IV proposed to Her Majesty, Queen Victoria, the establishment of a bishop to be the Protestant representative in the Holy City.[24] The British Parliament passed a Bishopric Law, stating the bishop's primary care was missionary; in particular, the bishop was to tend "to conversion of the Jews,[25] to their protection, and to their employment."[26] The first bishop *in* Jerusalem (rather than "of" Jerusalem, in deference to the Greek and Latin Patriarchs), Michael Alexander, was consecrated in 1841 and arrived in Jerusalem in 1842. In 1881, the Church of England and the Lutheran Church each went their own way and formed two bishoprics.[27] Each continued educational and charitable work, built churches, and began social service agencies still integral to the life of the Holy City.[28]

Ilan Pappe says that, by the early years of the twentieth century, Anglican schools — mostly in Jerusalem, Nablus, and Nazareth — were seedbeds of Palestinian nationalism.[29] The British "gave in to the teachers who wished to Arabize the Anglican colleges. The Anglican schools had been intended as purely missionary establishments but . . . passed into the hands of the Palestinian Native Church Council, an organization of Palestinian priests. . . ."[30] The concern of the Council, says Pappe, went beyond a missionary endeavor to "secularizing and politicizing the local educated elite." He goes on: ". . . St. George's College in Jerusalem deserves a particular place in the pantheon of formative national Palestinian institutions. The sons of Muslim elite attended this school in great numbers. . . . St. George's and its like in Jaffa, Haifa, Nablus, and Nazareth shaped the *Weltanschauung* of those who would form the social elite of the Palestinian national movement."[31]

The success of Anglican educational endeavors had an effect in the religious realm as well. Young Palestinian Christians who studied in Anglican schools often left Greek Orthodox and Catholic churches to join the Anglican Church, thereby exacerbating centuries-old conflicts among Christian churches, East and West.[32] But at the heart of these conflicts were conflicting claims to the Holy Places, specifically the Holy Sepulchre, Deir el-Sultan, adjacent to the Holy Sepulchre,[33] the Sanctuary of the Ascension on the Mount of Olives, the Tomb of the Virgin Mary in the Valley of Jehoshaphat, and the Church and Grotto of the Nativity in Bethlehem. As has been noted, these conflicts began in the Crusader era and were bitterly engaged throughout the four centuries of Ottoman rule.

The claims and counterclaims[34] by the churches were entangled in international politics, particularly in the nineteenth century. Latin claims were championed by France, while the Orthodox cause rallied around Russian ambitions.[35] Finally, in 1852, the Ottoman sultan issued a *firman*, or decision to define rights of pre-eminence to the Holy Places. The 1878 Treaty of Berlin[36] confirmed this definition, and it became and still is the Status Quo over the Holy Places in Jerusalem and Bethlehem. The Status Quo governs the time and manner of public worship at each altar, the decorations of altars or shrines, the use of lamps and tapestries and pictures, and acts of ownership, such as cleaning and repair.[37]

The Status Quo not only dealt with the claims of the Christian churches in relation to the Holy Places. It also guaranteed the rights and the freedoms of all Christian churches and all Christians in relation to the Holy Places: freedom of access to the Holy Places (meaning entry into the country as well as at doors and gates), freedom of religious worship, and so on.[38]

To acknowledge this unrelentingly conflictual history is to become aware of just how unprecedented it was, and is, for the Jerusalem Heads of Churches to issue these joint statements. Of course, there were indications of interchurch relations prior to January 1988 — for example, ecumenical worship services during the Week of Prayer for Christian Unity.[39] These initiatives were much strengthened by the visit of Pope Paul VI in 1964. The pope's visit was not only a pilgrimage to emphasize the importance of the Holy Places to the Vatican; the visit, scheduled during the years of the Second Vatican Council, was primarily intended to provide ecumenical encouragement to Christian leaders in the Holy Land. His meeting with, and embrace of, the Ecumenical Patriarch Athenagoras on the Mount of Olives on 6 January 1964 confirmed this intent.[40] Another indicator of the pope's intention to encourage ecumenicity was his strong support for a proposal made by two eminent Protestant observers at the Second Vatican Council — Oscar Cullmann and Kristen E. Skydsgaard — to found an ecumenical institute for advanced studies. There were a number of proposals for the location of such an institute; Pope Paul VI insisted that the ecumenical institute be located in Jerusalem.[41]

Yet, even as these ecumenical initiatives went forward, there were also indicators of latent, centuries-old conflict. While neither Greek Orthodox nor Catholics — the two main contestants for pre-eminence over the Holy Places, historically speaking — could (or can) imagine tampering with the Status Quo, the strict observance of every stipulation has been and remains a matter of mutual vigilance. Moreover, opposing interpretations of the definition of the "final *firman*" were and still are discussed, if not debated. Perhaps most pronounced is the not only lingering but living Greek Orthodox concern about proselytism.[42] As has been noted, although the nineteenth-century influx of Protestant and additional Catholic missionaries offered much-needed educational, medical, and material assistance to the local Christian communities, it often resulted in the conversion of the Palestinian Orthodox population. This concern, therefore, was well-founded; it continues to inform the hesitancy of the Greek Orthodox hierarchy to take local ecumenical initiatives.[43]

The joint statements by the Jerusalem Heads of Churches are also unprecedented in that they address political issues in public. On 27 June 1967, when the Christian Holy Places were under the rule of the State of Israel, the Knesset passed the "Protection of Holy Places Law": "The Holy Places shall be protected from desecration and any other violation and from anything likely to violate the freedom of access of the members of the different religions to the places sacred to them or their feelings with regard to those places."[44] The Israeli government also undertook negotiated agreements with Jerusalem churches, beginning with negotiations with the Vatican in July 1967. Bilateral agreements between Jerusalem churches and the Israeli government continued through the seventies and into the eighties, agreements that emphasized the terms of the Status Quo and focused on the preservation of the Holy Places, freedom of access to all persons, and the rights of religious communities living in the Holy Land.[45] These bilateral agreements tended to perpetuate obtuse patterns of interaction that finally forged the Status Quo, patterns also tangled in a tradition of *divide et impera,* "divide and rule," that tended to marginalize churches relative to civil authorities.[46]

By issuing public statements to address political as well as pastoral issues, Jerusalem churches initiated a new way of relating to civil authorities. The churches moved into a more engaged relationship and took a more prophetic stance. As will be noted in Chapter One, this shift meant a shake-up in church-state relations.[47]

What, then, enabled the Jerusalem Heads of Churches to take this unprecedented action? I suggest two factors: the "decolonization" or indigenization of church leadership, and the beginning of the first Intifada. The process of indigenization of local church leaders began in 1979, when the Evangelical Lutheran Church consecrated Daoud S. Haddad on

31 October 1979 at the Church of the Redeemer in Jerusalem. In 1984, Samir Kaf'ity was consecrated as twelfth Anglican Bishop in Jerusalem. Perhaps most significantly, on 6 January 1988, Michel Asa'ad Sabbah, a native of Nazareth, was consecrated to be the new Latin Patriarch.[48] The first joint public statement by the Jerusalem Heads of Churches — "The recent painful events in our Land . . . are a clear indication of the grievous suffering of our people on the West Bank and in the Gaza Strip" — was issued a few weeks later, on 22 January 1988.

As noted above, this first statement was issued in response to the eruption — a word often used in histories of the first Intifada in early December 1987. The imperative for church leaders to speak was strengthened by the fact that this uprising was a thoroughly popular uprising. Palestinians from all walks of life — shopkeepers, construction workers, intellectuals, women and men, young and old — joined the "children of stones"[49] who revived the struggle for the liberation of Palestine. Therefore, "We, the Heads of the Christian Communities in Jerusalem, . . . take our stand with truth and justice against all forms of injustice and oppression."

As I read and re-read, and read again, these statements by the Jerusalem Heads of Churches, a four-chapter outline emerged. These chapters begin with a context-setting essay, followed by the statements.

A word about the statements themselves — they are stylistically inconsistent. For example, the titles of the Heads of Churches occasionally vary. I present the statements essentially in the form in which I found them. Many I found in English, the language in which they were initially written. They were then translated into Arabic and French. Some statements I found only in the French translation; these I had professionally retranslated into English.[50] A few statements I found only in fragmentary or in summary form. These are included, and I have indicated their fragmentary or summary status.

And so, *Jerusalem Testament: Palestinian Christians Speak, 1988-2008.*

ONE   "We . . . Stand with Truth and Justice"

(1988-1992)

Intifada

The first Intifada — in Arabic, "a shaking off" — began on 9 December 1987, the day after an Israeli army tank-transport truck hit a minibus carrying laborers who were returning home after a day's work in Israel. The minibus was stopped at a checkpoint. Four of the passengers were killed immediately; seven others were badly injured. Fatal traffic accidents are not uncommon in the Gaza Strip, or elsewhere in Israel. However, the response to this fatal traffic accident was a spontaneous combustion. Rumors were rife that this was not an accident, but rather a cold-blooded act of vengeful retaliation by the relative of an Israeli labor contractor who had been stabbed to death on 7 December.

The traffic accident lit the smoldering anger and resentment over twenty years of occupation — the confiscation of tens of thousands of acres of land, the illegal[1] settlements built on this land, the denial of human and civil rights, the administrative detentions, the taxation to subsidize military occupation, the house demolitions, the separation of families, the closures and checkpoints that restrict freedom of movement, the collective punishments such as twenty-four-hour curfews, and on and on — begun after the humiliating debacle of the Six-Day War in 1967.

The tinderbox of occupation was stoked by years of Palestinians' dispossession and dispersal as refugees after *al Nakba,* the Catastrophe of 1948. It is not at all incidental that the Intifada began in a refugee camp, the

Jabalya refugee camp, where 65,000 women, men, and children live on half a square mile of sandy soil. And it is not surprising that *shabab*,[2] the young men and women[3] in the Palestinian refugee camps and villages and towns of the Occupied Territories, were the activist core of the Intifada. These were, and are, places where destroyed homes and villages were, and are, named as living memory, still "living stones" of destroyed villages. These were, and are, the places where the children's identity as Palestinians who rightfully belonged to this land has been nurtured. These children became the "children of stones," the *shabab* who revived the struggle for the liberation of Palestine. They led the way, and soon the whole people joined in an uprising.

The uprising was not altogether unprecedented. There had been earlier uprisings and revolts. In 1834, at a time when the Ottoman rulers lost control of Syria and Palestine, the upstart Egyptian governor Muhammad Ali occupied the provinces and enforced quotas for conscripts for military service. In 1929, a local dispute over worship arrangements at the Wailing Wall in Jerusalem spilled into streets all over the country, especially in the more mixed Jewish and Palestinian towns of Hebron in the south and Safed in the north. And from 1936 to 1939, there was the Great Arab Revolt against the British Mandate and its apparent allowance of waves of Jewish immigration.[4]

But this uprising, this shaking off, was distinct. David McDowell comments, "The Uprising . . . unified people to an unprecedented extent. Its direction, authority, and impetus were rooted in the experience of the common people. This was a new sensation of Palestinian nationalism."[5] Most radical and significant, as Avi Shlaim (among others) points out, was that the first Intifada "had already begun to embody the Palestinian state and to build its institutions and infrastructure."[6] At the heart of this infrastructure were locally organized popular committees. The committees distributed food and medical supplies, coordinated schools that met underground because regular schools were closed, and organized demonstrations. Most strategically, the committees enabled Palestinians to "disengage from the Israeli system, economically and administratively, and to effect a simultaneous takeover of the control of [their] daily activities."[7] This grassroots, nonviolent[8] uprising animated the Palestinian people as a whole people; it involved all ages, classes, and faith communities, both rural and urban populations. In the words of Father Frans Bouwen, a Belgian White Father (Pere Blanc) who has lived for more than forty years in

St. Anne's[9] just inside the Lion's Gate to the Old City of Jerusalem, the Palestinian people were finally "liberated from fear."

This liberation from fear, this uprising, defined the political context in which the Heads of Churches in Jerusalem published a first joint statement on 22 January 1988:

> We, the Heads of the Christian Communities in Jerusalem, would like to express in all honesty and clarity that we take our stand with truth and justice against all forms of injustice and oppression. We stand with the suffering and the oppressed. . . . We call upon the faithful to pray and to labor for justice and peace for all the people of our area. And in response to the same Word of God, prompted by our faith in God and our Christian duty, we have decided to call upon all our sons and daughters who are with us . . . to give expression to what we feel we ought to do in these ways.

The Jerusalem Heads of Churches then call the faithful to pray for justice and peace during the Week of Prayer for Christian Unity, to dedicate 29 January as a "day for fasting and self-denial, . . . and to give what you thus save towards the support of our needy brothers and sisters," and so on, so that "peace [will] permeate our country and the song of the angels on the birthday of Jesus Christ, the 'King of Peace,' [will] be a reality. 'Glory to God in the highest, and on earth peace, good will towards men.'"

Like many of the statements that followed, this first statement was written to be read aloud to the gathered faithful. The Heads of Churches addressed "our people"; they spoke primarily pastorally. They also spoke as "Spiritual Leaders" in solidarity with "our people" and thus represented them to prime ministers and presidents, and to the United Nations, the international community, and churches throughout the world. This dual pastoral/spiritual leader voice can be clearly heard in this excerpt from the 27 April 1989 statement:

> It is our Christian conviction that as Spiritual Leaders we have an urgent duty to follow up the developments in this situation and to make known to the world the conditions of life of our people here in the Holy Land. In Jerusalem, on the West Bank and in Gaza our people experience in their daily lives constant deprivation of their fundamental rights because of arbitrary actions deliberately taken by the authorities. Our people are often subjected to unprovoked harassment and hardship.

The Heads of Churches in Jerusalem go on to give examples of the "unprovoked harassment and hardship" — for example, loss of lives, particularly of children's lives, shooting incidents in the vicinity of the Holy Places, "harsh curfew causing considerable economic stress and human hardship," mass administrative arrests, detentions without trial, and collective punishment, including house demolitions, deprivation of basic services such as supplying water and electricity, and closure of schools and universities.[10]

A major incidence of "harassment and hardship" prompted the publication of another statement six months later. The statement of 26 October 1989 addressed the dire situation in Beit Sahour, one of three traditionally Christian villages just south of Jerusalem: Bethlehem, Beit Jala to the west, and Beit Sahour, site of the Shepherds' Fields, to the east. Beit Sahour residents, pointing to the deteriorated state of their roads, their inferior school, the absence of basic services, and their limited access to medical care, declared that their taxes were unfair. In mid-1988, the entire village of Beit Sahour decided to refuse to pay taxes to Israel; by September 1989, Israel moved to suppress this classic nonviolent protest with a harsh military crackdown. What is referred to as the siege of Beit Sahour began on 22 September 1989 and ended on 31 October 1989. During the first days of the siege, the village was placed under twenty-four-hour curfew and declared a closed military zone. For the rest of the siege the curfew began at five P.M. and was lifted twelve hours later. Telephone lines were cut. Many residents were arrested. Homes and stores were ransacked as tax authorities confiscated and auctioned furniture and other possessions, far in excess of the value of taxes said to be owed. In his account of the tax revolt and the subsequent siege, Charles Sennott notes that, from the perspective of the Palestinians, the taxes they paid were "actually funding the Israeli military administration. . . . It was worse than taxation without representation; it was taxation with occupation, and the Beit Sahourans didn't see the wisdom in underwriting their own oppression."[11]

The Heads of Churches responded to this siege in the 26 October statement: "[We] who are the spiritual fathers of the people and share the suffering of those afflicted express their growing concern and call all believers to pray with them for peace and justice." And again, just as the Heads of Churches had called for concrete action to accompany words in their first statement of 22 January 1988, the very next day after the publication of this October 1989 statement, the three Patriarchs (Greek, Latin, and

Armenian), together with the Most Reverend Father Custos[12] and the Greek Catholic Patriarchal Vicar Monsignor Lufti Laham, organized a convoy and traveled together to Beit Sahour. They were accompanied by two wagons of food. The convoy was stopped by a military roadblock at Rachel's Tomb, just at the entry to Bethlehem. Undeterred, the convoy turned around and went back toward Jerusalem, then turned west and went around through Beit Jala and so back into Bethlehem, where the Heads of Churches visited the Church of the Nativity and the Latin Parish Church of St. Catherine, in each of which they prayed together. They met the Israeli army again right in front of the Basilica, where they were told they could enter Beit Sahour only in one car escorted by the army chief. The Heads of Churches did not accept this condition. Still undeterred, they made their way to the Mar Elias Monastery on the road to Jerusalem to pray.

This experience was especially profound for the Greek Orthodox Patriarch, who, until this incident, had been rather sheltered, shielded, from such harassment, and who came from an ecclesial sensibility that assumed church-state consonance. Rather defiantly undeterred, two days later he managed to get into Beit Sahour to pray with his people, and also with the Latin Christian community there.[13] After the siege was lifted, Palestinians gathered for an ecumenical service to give thanks. They invited Israeli peace activists who had supported their tax resistance to join them.

By mid-1990, tensions were heightened by the continuing Intifada and the presence of American troops in nearby Saudi Arabia, in response to Saddam Hussein's invasion of Kuwait. Then, during the festival of Sukkot in October 1990, a Jewish nationalist named Gershon Salomon, leader of the Faithful of the Temple Mount, or Temple Mount Loyalists, went with a group toward the Temple Mount, known as the Haram al-Sharif to Muslims. Salomon was blocked from the area, but, with tensions high, rocks flew and bullets were fired. Seventeen Palestinians were killed by Israeli police. There were several violent incidents involving Hamas[14] that followed in November and December. This escalation of violence was made worse by the outbreak of the Gulf War in January 1991. Just before the bombing began, on 12 January 1991, the Heads of Jerusalem sent a letter to Presidents Bush and Hussein: "We pray that you will decide for peace and relieve the current anxiety in the hearts of children, women, and men of all nations. 'Blessed are the peacemakers.'"

15

Church-State Shake-up

It was inevitable that the publication of joint statements by the Heads of Churches in Jerusalem would have some consequence in relation to the Israeli government.[15] Before this newly coordinated initiative, each church had related to the Israeli government bilaterally — that is, one on one. Moreover, these relationships varied. The coming together of the Heads of Churches to make a coordinated response to what was happening to the Palestinian people, to "our people," was unprecedented.[16] In a real sense, whether intentional or not, the newly coordinated approach by the Heads of Churches mirrored the "unified leadership" of the Intifada; a shadowy group, "the Unified Leadership of the Uprising" (UNLU) included representatives of all the major political factions,[17] all of whom were inhabitants of the Occupied Territories. The Israelis, try as they might, could not locate it. The leadership's strategy was to stay on the move and issue intermittent, mimeographed leaflets or communiqués, directives, *bayans*, with information and instructions to implement a unified political program of action. For example, they announced strike days and boycotts, as well as proclaiming and shaping the opinion of a newly organized people. The language of the leaflets was stirring in its rhetoric, which was both political and poetic.[18]

In this political situation and with their own similarly unified strategy, which also involved issuing statements, the Heads of Churches were not at all sure what response they would get from civil authorities. Michael Dumper, commenting on the earliest statements, says they were "tentative and cautious in their support for the Palestinian intifada. Their support was couched in general terms."[19] Father Frans Bouwen more sympathetically points out that, precisely because they were unsure of the response of the Israeli government, they were testing the waters.[20] This relative tentativeness may also be indicated by the fact that the first two statements (issued on 22 January 1988 and 25 April 1988) are "signed" by offices; no names are given. Nonetheless, as Dumper himself notes, it was "particularly significant"[21] that, after the first two, subsequent early statements were signed by the heads of the major Christian communities: His Beatitude Diodoros I, Greek Orthodox Patriarch; His Beatitude Michel Sabbah, Latin Patriarch; Bishop Samir Kaf'ity, President Bishop of the Episcopal Church in Jerusalem and the Middle East; Archbishop Lufti Laham, Patriarchal Vicar of the Greek Catholic Church; His Beatitude Yeghishe Derderian, Armenian Orthodox Patriarch; Bishop Naim Nassar, Evangelical Lutheran Church in Jordan; His Beatitude Basilios, Coptic Orthodox Patriarch; Archbishop Dionysios Behnam Jijjawi, Syrian Orthodox Bishop Patriarchal Vicar; and the Most Reverend Father Cechitelli (O.F.M.), Custos of the Holy Land. Later statements were also signed by the Ethiopian Orthodox archbishop of Jerusalem.

Were there consequences for church-state relations? It is, of course, difficult to ascribe cause and effect. There were, however, several incidents that may indicate increasing stress in church-state relations. The most egregious incident took place on 11 April 1990, when the Greek Orthodox property St. John's Hospice (just off the Muritan Square, adjoining the Church of the Holy Sepulchre) was occupied by 150 armed Jewish settlers affiliated with Ateret Cohanim ("the priests' diadem"). Ateret Cohanim is a settler group, founded in 1978 by disciples of Rabbi Tzvi Yehuda Kook, whose dual purpose is to train priests in the offering of animal sacrifices in preparation for rites at a Solomonic altar of a rebuilt Temple and to acquire property in the Old City of Jerusalem, in both the Christian and the Muslim Quarters. The group is clear that its overall purpose is to transform Jerusalem into a holy city prepared to serve the Third Temple. The timing of the occupation — during Holy Week — was particularly provocative, as was the fact that it was "coupled with the very public humiliation of the [Greek] patriarch being tear-gassed and knocked to the ground by a gang of squatters."[22] Nur Masalha reports, "On 27 April 1990, all the major Christian churches in Israel and the Occupied Territories closed and rang funeral peals in protest. It was the first time that the Church of the Holy Sepulchre had been closed in eight hundred years."[23]

The Israeli government did not intervene; indeed, there was what Dumper calls "a bitter exchange of letters between the patriarch and the president of Israel."[24] The significance of the incident is magnified by the fact that the matter is still in the process of litigation in Israeli courts. The former secretary to the Armenian Orthodox Patriarch, Kevork Hintlian, articulated the sentiment of many Christians when he said, "The Christian Quarter after April 11th is not the same Christian Quarter before then."[25] Dumper comments, "The incident was probably the most serious in church-state relations since 1967, with ramifications that are still being played out today."[26]

The statements published between January 1988 and December 1992 mention other incidents that may indicate stress in church-state relationships. These include the imposition of municipal and state taxes on church properties, an issue that also continues to be negotiated; encroachment on church land; acts of "desecration" and acts of vandalism in the Holy Sepulchre; patriarchs and heads of churches being "targets of attacks by Israeli Officials and the Israeli media"; "the stabbing of the Patriarchal Vicar of the Syrian Catholic Church" on Christmas Eve 1991; slashed tires on cars parked beside church properties; and difficulty with maintenance of the "Historical Rights" of the churches, including limited "free access to the Holy Places on occasion." All of this, in the words of the 23 April 1990 statement, "threatens the survival of the Christian community in the Holy City," and, in the words of the 23 March 1991 statement, is "an attempt to change the unique and pluralistic character of Jerusalem."[27]

Yet another indicator of a church-state shake-up is a matter addressed already in the second joint public statement by the Heads of Churches in Jerusalem: the presence of "the so-called 'Christian Embassy.'" The "most influential and controversial"[28] of Christian Zionist organizations, the International Christian Embassy, Jerusalem (ICEJ), burst onto the political and religious scene in 1980, inspired by the Knesset's unilateral declaration of Jerusalem as the eternal and undivided capital of Israel. The response to the Knesset's action was worldwide condemnation. In counter-response, Christian Zionists met in Jerusalem and founded the ICEJ to demonstrate solidarity with the beleaguered State of Israel. The decision, said the founder, Jan Willem van der Hoeven, was "a direct response to the world's cowardice,"[29] particularly the cowardice of countries who moved their embassies from Jerusalem to Tel Aviv. The highest priority of the ICEJ is to be "a focus of comfort" to "the reborn state of Israel."[30] In sum, says Stephen Sizer, the founding of the ICEJ "represented the coming of age of Christian Zionism as a high profile, politically astute, international movement."[31]

But, declared the Heads of Churches in their 25 April 1988 statement, the ICEJ "does not represent or replace the Christian community in Jerusalem or the majority of the Faithful all over the world. We do not acknowledge this body or its activities and conferences. The teachings of our Lord and the light of the Gospel have gone out from this very Holy Land. We are the representatives of Christianity here, venerating and safeguarding the Holy Places. . . ." The significance of this statement has become steadily clearer through the nearly twenty years since it was made, inasmuch as it has become the Israeli government's procedure, if not policy, to privilege international Christian bodies, particularly Christian Zionist bodies, and, accordingly, to sideline the local historic churches.[32]

Peace "based on justice and truth for all"

As the Intifada lengthened, living conditions inside the Occupied Territories had seriously deteriorated as a result of Israeli pressures, pressures the United States steadfastly refused to condemn. Then, in May 1990, the United States vetoed a U.N. resolution calling for an observer force in the West Bank and Gaza after an Israeli reservist killed seven Palestinian workers in a settlement that month. According to Sara Roy, this was the point at which the Palestinians turned to Iraq. Roy states, "Vocal and widespread Palestinian support of Saddam Hussein was therefore not triggered by Iraq's invasion of Kuwait, but by U.S. intervention in the region and by the double standards in the treatment of the Palestinian issue that were subsequently highlighted."[33] Against this backdrop — the Temple Mount massacre in October 1990, escalating violence in November and December, the outbreak of the Gulf War in January 1991, and consequent shifting geopolitical alignments[34] — it became clear that peace talks were imperative.[35]

The Madrid Peace Conference — the first conference at which Palestinians were represented "on a footing of equality with Israel"[36] — was convened in October 1991. The Jerusalem Heads of Churches sent a message to the delegates of the Madrid Peace Conference: "We all face the challenge to be peacemakers. We repeat our deep commitment and pastoral concern for the welfare of all peoples in this land. . . . We call upon all parties concerned to remember that all people carry the same image and likeness of God and are children of the same Lord. . . . We assure you of our constant prayers. . . . We pray that you will be guided to lay the foundation for a peaceful resolution of the Middle East conflict based on justice and truth for all."

The Jerusalem Heads of Churches Speak

··

22 January 1988–December 1992

Jerusalem, 22nd of January, 1988

To all our sons and daughters, our sisters and brothers in the Holy Land.

"Thus says the Lord: Let not the wise man glory in his wisdom, let not the mighty man glory in his might, let not the rich man glory in his riches: but let him who glories glory in this, that he understands and knows me, that I am the Lord who practices kindness, justice, and righteousness in the earth: for in these things I delight, says the Lord" (Jeremiah 9:23-24).

The recent painful events in our Land which have resulted in so many victims, both killed and wounded, are a clear indication of the grievous suffering of our people on the West Bank and in the Gaza Strip. They are also a visible expression of our people's aspirations to achieve their legal rights and the realization of their hopes.

We, the Heads of the Christian Communities in Jerusalem, would like to express in all honesty and clarity that we take our stand with truth and justice against all forms of injustice and oppression. We stand with the suffering and the oppressed, we stand with the refugees and the deported, with the distressed and the victims of injustice, we stand with those who mourn and are bereaved, with the hungry and the poor. In accordance with the Word of God through the prophet Isaiah, chapter 1, verse 17:

"Learn to do good; seek justice; correct oppression; defend the fatherless; plead for the widow."

We call upon the faithful to pray and to labor for justice and peace for all the people of our area.

And in response to the same Word of God, prompted by our faith in God and our Christian duty, we have decided to call upon all our sons and daughters who are with us, an integral part of the people of this Holy Land who are laboring and witnessing for justice and peace, to give expression to what we feel we ought to do in these ways:

1. We call upon all our sons and daughters to pray for justice and peace for our Land and for all its peoples throughout this Week of Prayer: Sunday, 24 January, to Sunday, 31 January 1988.
2. We call upon faithful Christians to dedicate next Friday, 29 January 1988, as a day for fasting and self-denial, identifying ourselves with our brothers and sisters in the camps on the West Bank and in the Gaza Strip. We request you to give what you thus save towards the support of our needy brothers and sisters, remembering that Friday speaks to us of the passion of our Lord Jesus Christ, of his crucifixion, and of his death to redeem all humanity.
3. We have resolved to set apart Sunday, 31 January, in all the churches of our various communities as a day of prayer and preaching when fervent prayer will be offered in the regular worship services, that justice and peace may be realized in our Land, so that all may live there in safety, security, and peace. At the end of these services, donations towards the support of our needy brothers and sisters will be collected.

We solemnly charge the Christian faithful to fill the churches by their presence, and actively to contribute to the success of what we intend to do, praying that God may inspire and direct all leaders and people in authority to bring to reality what all of us hope and work for so that the foundations of truth, justice, and peace may be firmly laid in our beloved part of the world.

Therefore, we again state unequivocally that all our Christian Churches in this country, standing together, seek real peace based on justice and which will never be established unless every person's rights are fully respected: only when this happens will crises cease, peace permeate our country, and the song of the angels on the birthday of Jesus Christ, "the King of Peace," be a reality.

"Glory to God in the highest, and on earth, peace, good will towards men."

The Greek Orthodox Patriarchate
The Latin Patriarchate
The Armenian Patriarchate
The Syrian Orthodox Bishopric
The Greek Catholic (Melkite) Bishopric
The Anglican Bishopric
The Lutheran Bishopric
The Syrian Catholic Church
The Franciscan Custody of the Holy Land

About the So-called "Christian Embassy"

The Christian Churches in the Holy Land, whose roots go back to the beginning of Christianity, hereby state the following:

1. The so-called "Christian Embassy" does not represent nor replace the Christian community in Jerusalem or the majority of the Faithful all over the world. We do not acknowledge this body nor its activities and conferences. The teachings of our Lord and the light of the Gospel have gone out from this very Holy Land. We are the representatives of Christianity here, venerating and safeguarding the Holy Places, and we do not expect people coming from abroad, unaware of our problems, to act on our behalf.
2. We categorically refuse and reject any political interpretation of the Holy Scripture.
3. According to our Lord's commands, we seek peace and justice for all the people of the world, and especially in the region, without any kind of discrimination or violence.

Heads of Churches in Jerusalem
Greek Orthodox Patriarchate
Latin Patriarchate
Armenian Orthodox Bishopric
Syrian Orthodox Bishopric
Anglican Bishopric
Lutheran Bishopric
Syrian Catholic Church
Holy Land Franciscans (Custody of the Holy Land)

Jerusalem, 25 April 1988

Statement by the Heads of the Christian Communities in Jerusalem

We, the Heads of the Christian Communities in the Holy City, have met together in view of the grave situation prevailing in Jerusalem and the whole of our country.

It is our Christian conviction that as Spiritual Leaders we have an urgent duty to follow up the developments of this situation and to make known to the world the conditions of life of our people here in the Holy Land.

In Jerusalem, on the West Bank and in Gaza our people experience in their daily lives constant deprivation of their fundamental rights because of arbitrary actions deliberately taken by the authorities. Our people are often subjected to unprovoked harassment and hardship.

We are particularly concerned by the tragic and unnecessary loss of Palestinian lives, especially among minors. Unarmed and innocent people are being killed by the unwarranted use of firearms, and hundreds are wounded by the excessive use of force.

We protest against the frequent shooting incidents in the vicinity of the Holy Places.

We also condemn the practice of mass administrative arrests, and of continuing detention of adults and minors without trial. We further condemn the use of all forms of collective punishment, including the demolition of homes and depriving whole communities of basic services such as water and electricity.

We appeal to the world community to support our demand for the re-opening of schools and universities, closed for the past sixteen months, so that thousands of our children can enjoy again their basic right to education.

We demand that the authorities respect the right of believers to enjoy free access to all places of worship on the Holy Days of all our religions.

We affirm our human solidarity and sympathy with all who are suffering and oppressed; we pray for the return of peace based on justice to Jerusalem and the Holy Land; and we request the international community and the United Nations Organization to give urgent attention to the plight of the Palestinian people, and to work for a speedy and just resolution of the Palestinian problem.

Jerusalem, 27th April 1989

Signed:
H.B. Diodoros I — Greek Orthodox Patriarch of Jerusalem
H.B. Michel Sabbah — Latin Patriarch of Jerusalem
Bishop Samir Kafity — President Bishop, Episcopal Church in
    Jerusalem and the Middle East
Archbishop Lutfi Laham — Patriarchal Vicar, Greek Catholic
    Patriarchate of Jerusalem
H.B. Yeghishe Derderian — Armenian Orthodox Patriarch of
    Jerusalem
Bishop Naim Nassar — Evangelical Lutheran Church in Jordan
H.B. Basilios — Coptic Orthodox Patriarch of Jerusalem
Archbishop Dionysios Behnam Jijjawi — Syrian Orthodox
    Patriarchal Vicar of Jerusalem
Most Rev. Father Cechitelli (O.F.M.) — Custos of the Holy Land

Press Release

Following the last meeting, held on April 26th, 1989, during which a declaration of the Heads of the Churches was issued expressing deep concern over the prevailing situation in the West Bank and the Gaza Strip, their Beatitudes Diodoros I, the Greek Orthodox Patriarch of Jerusalem, Michel

Sabbah, the Latin Patriarch of Jerusalem, and Yeghishe Derderian, the Armenian Patriarch of Jerusalem, and the Very Reverend Fr. Carlo Cechitelli, Custos of the Holy Land, met today on the 26th [of] October 1989 to review the aggravating situation in the above-mentioned areas and the new methods used against the population in Beit Sahour.

During this meeting:

1. They express satisfaction for the efforts which are being made all over the world to reach a settlement for the Middle East question.
2. They feel disappointed with the general deterioration of the situation in the life of the population on the West Bank and Gaza Strip since their meeting of 26th April 1989.
3. They consider what is going on in Beit Sahour for the last forty days, and which is causing undue suffering to the population, as unjust and unacceptable.
4. The Patriarchs, who are the spiritual fathers of the people and share the suffering of those who are afflicted, express their growing concern and call all believers to pray with them for peace and justice.
5. They ask their respective communities to hold special prayers on Sunday, 29 October 1989, for the sufferings in the West Bank and Gaza Strip and for the population of Beit Sahour in their particular situation.
6. They will send food supplies for the population of Beit Sahour.
7. They decide to follow up the situation with all appropriate means at their disposal.

26th October 1989

Christmas 1989 Statement by the Jerusalem Heads of Churches

To our beloved children in the Lord.

As we approach the third Christmas under the present difficult and trying conditions, we, the spiritual Heads of the Christian Communities, wish to address our compassionate greetings to our children in the Holy Land, who experience times of great injustice and violence.

We remind the world of our solidarity and sympathy with the victims of violence. We wish to tell to the world that we are witnessing an escalation in the sad events and there are omens of a human tragedy unfolding in the coming year; hence our appeal to all concerned and to the world.

As we live these moments of despair and tragedy, the message of "peace on earth" which was proclaimed from the fields of Bethlehem brings consolation and a ray of hope to all the afflicted and suffering.

Jesus Christ, "the Prince of Peace," through His Incarnation calls all people in this Land to reconcile in mutual love and respect, based on justice and reciprocal tolerance.

"Peace on Earth" is possible only when all people and states concerned recognize the legitimate rights of all individuals and nations to freedom and self-determination.

Specifically today, when the Superpowers are heading for global reconciliation, we appeal to the leaders of the world to give urgent attention to the pressing, painful problem in the Holy Land. We, the spiritual Heads of the Christian Communities, are called by our Lord to stand by those who suffer from injustice and pray for the establishment of justice and peaceful settlement of the conflict.

In this spirit, we condemn all manifestations of violence, [and] indiscriminate use of force, [which] we have witnessed almost every day during the last two years.

We grieve with the families who have lost their beloved ones, and we pray God to alleviate the suffering of the wounded and the prisoners.

We expect . . . the Leaders and concerned Authorities to show timely courage and wisdom in solving the painful problem of this land to the mutual benefit of both nations.

We address . . . both peoples in the area, despite . . . the sufferings they are passing through, to prepare themselves for reconciliation and love towards one another.

Pray to the Lord to strengthen us in hope and love to carry our burden as Shepherds of our people . . . that soon we will witness the end of human suffering and bloodshed in this Land of Peace, so that all of us together may glorify the name of the Lord.

May the divine Infant of Bethlehem bless you on this Christmas time and all through the new year 1990.

Statement Release (fragment)

We, the Patriarchs, the Custos, and the Heads of the Churches and Christian Communities of Jerusalem, have gathered together today, April 23, 1990, to formulate our response to the extremely serious events that took place during Holy Week and the consequences that followed.

On the afternoon of April 11, 1990, Wednesday of Holy Week, 150 settlers, among whom numbered many armed men, forcibly took Saint John's Hospice, located in the heart of the Christian Quarter in the Old City, a 3,000 square-meter property belonging to the Greek Orthodox Patriarchate.

Their act was supported by Israeli authorities. It was financed, at least in large part, by the government, and there have been visits from government ministers and parliamentary officials to encourage the settlers. It appears that later on, high-level government officials interceded to prevent the police from enforcing court orders for eviction.

This act took place just before the culmination of Holy Week and unfortunately led to the interruption of some of the most solemn ceremonies of the Christian religion in the most sacred sanctuary of Christianity, the Basilica of the Holy Sepulchre.

The government-backed act of the settlers continues to provoke daily violence within the neighborhood around Saint Sepulchre, where administrative centers for the Churches are situated; it has occasioned the provocative presence of a large number of armed men within a confined space. Consequently, freedom of access to Saint Sepulchre and the freedom of the area in general are now threatened.

This act of armed settlement seriously compromises the integrity and the cultural and religious autonomy of the Christian, Armenian, and Muslim neighborhoods and is in violation of the secular status and character of these neighborhoods of the Holy City, which have been respected by all who have ruled Jerusalem in the past and by the international community (and which the Israeli authorities themselves have promised to safeguard on numerous occasions).[37]

Furthermore, this action constitutes a danger to the survival of all Christian communities within the Holy City.

We, the Heads of the Christian Churches and Communities of Jerusalem, unreservedly condemn the actions of these settlers.

We deplore the open support and encouragement that this action has received from Israeli government quarters.

We ask that Israeli authorities arrange for the immediate evacuation of these settlers and return the property to its legitimate owners, the Greek Orthodox Patriarchate.

We call upon the international community, upon all the Churches, upon all religious leaders, and upon all men of goodwill throughout the world to lend us their active support.

We have unanimously decided that:

1. On Friday, April 27, all the Christian Holy Places in Jerusalem, Nazareth, Bethlehem, and elsewhere in the Holy Land shall close their doors at nine a.m. and shall not re-open until the next day.
2. On the same day, Churches throughout the country shall toll their bells once per hour between nine a.m. and noon.
3. Sunday, April 29, shall be a special day of prayer focusing on the Christian community of Jerusalem. We invite all our Christian brothers throughout the world to join us.

We have decided to remain in open session in order to closely follow the developments in this affair.

Greek Orthodox Patriarch of Jerusalem
Latin Patriarch of Jerusalem
Armenian Patriarch of Jerusalem
Custos of the Holy Land (Franciscan)
Coptic Archbishop of Jerusalem
Syrian Archbishop of Jerusalem
Ethiopian Archbishop of Jerusalem
Anglican Bishop in Jerusalem
Greek-Catholic Patriarchal Vicar
Lutheran Bishop of Jerusalem

Pentecost 1990: Christians for Peace in the Holy Land

Pentecost Prayer from Jerusalem

O Holy Spirit, tongue of fire, descend upon us as you descended upon the disciples gathered in the Upper Room for prayers. Sanctify us, free us from the bondage of sin, and give us your power to speak with one voice.

Rushing wind, sweep over our lands and make your sound gather again devout people from every nation under heaven. Help us manifest together the victory of life over death given through the Resurrection. Make us signs of the Living Hope and witnesses of Your peace.

Giver of life, abide in us, transform our former selves into a new life in faithfulness to God's will. Along with all the others with whom we live, with all nations and peoples we would enter a new time, a time of transformation when hatred is replaced by love, violence by dialogue, condemnation by forgiveness, self-centeredness by sharing.

Power of unity, help us to move from the Babel of division due to ethnic or religious boundaries to the Pentecost of unity in the diversity of our gifts, traditions, and cultures. Make us ministers of reconciliation among all the children of Abraham.

Spirit of truth, free us from our alienation from you. Liberate us from the powers and principalities which oppress and alienate. Make us instruments of Your justice to which we have been called by prophets, apostles, and martyrs.

Jesus is risen. The splendor of His realm is through your power, O Holy Spirit, available to all. Make us messengers of the Good News, apostles of the peace of Jerusalem, the peace of the Holy Land, the peace of the whole world.

Blessed are the peacemakers, for they shall be called children of God (Matthew 5:9).

3 June 1990

Statement Release (fragment)

We, the Christian Communities of Jerusalem, deeply share the pain and suffering that befell our people as a result of the tragic events that took place at 11 o'clock on the morning of October 8, 1990, at the al-Haram al-Sharif[38] and the Wailing Wall, during which dozens of individuals were killed and a great many were injured.[39]

We can only condemn this massacre and want to stress that we should never allow the creation of an atmosphere that can lead to conflict and confrontation among the believers of the three monotheistic faiths.

We offer condolences to the families of the victims and pray to God that the reasons for this conflict can end and that truth, justice, and peace can prevail.

8 October 1990

CHRISTMAS MESSAGE and STATEMENT by the PATRIARCHS and the HEADS of the CHURCHES in the HOLY LAND

We, the Patriarchs and the Heads of the Christian Churches in Jerusalem, have met today, when our region is living one of its most crucial crises in its modern history, dangerously poised on the brink of a devastating war.

We, the Spiritual Heads of the Christian Communities in the Holy Land, call upon the world leaders to follow the course of negotiation and peace and spare the region from ultimate destruction.

We deplore the fact that the Patriarchs and the Heads of the Christian Churches in the Holy Land are constant targets of attacks by Israeli Officials and the Israeli media. We consider it our sacred duty to voice our concern about human rights violations in the Occupied Territories, and everywhere, as well as with Jews in Israel. We call upon all parties to reconcile, forgive, and love each other. We call upon the responsibles to follow the path of negotiation rather than violence.

The prospects of constructive dialogue and peace in the Holy Land are receding. Despair is the pervasive mood.

We are witnessing a deterioration in the condition of the Palestinian people. There is considerable suffering and loss of lives. We pray for a quick reconciliation and a just settlement of the conflict.

As we look back at the past year, we witness that the local Church had to cope with a host of problems of a new nature:

> Constant attempts to change the demographic character of the Old City of Jerusalem, for example, the forcible and continuing seizure by "Ateret Cohanim" settlers of the St. John's Hospice (property of the Greek Orthodox Patriarchate).
>
> Continuing erosion of the traditional rights and centuries-old privileges of the Churches. Municipal and state taxes are being imposed on the Churches, in addition to encroachment on church land and properties, thus endangering its very survival.

We express our deep concern for the new problems confronting the local Church. They interfere with the proper functioning of our religious institutions, and we call upon the civil authorities in the country to safeguard our historic rights and status honored by all governments.

We ask our sons and daughters to join us in fervent prayer on Christmas Night; may the Lord grant us patience, strength, and love.

In view of the continuing sad state of affairs in our land, we have decided to restrict Christmas festivities to religious ceremonies, without any manifestation of joy, and devote our prayers [to] the peace of the Land and the world. Furthermore, all exchange visits between the Communities are cancelled.

Once more, we launch an urgent appeal from Bethlehem to all peace-loving people to influence their leaders to resolve the conflict in the Gulf without bloodshed and enormous loss of human lives.

We pray to the Lord to guide the leaders of the world in the path of peace and justice, and we pray for a year free of the threat of war and violence, extending our blessing to all the faithful.

> Greek Orthodox Patriarch of Jerusalem
> Latin Patriarch of Jerusalem
> Armenian Patriarch of Jerusalem
> Custos of the Holy Land (Franciscan)
> Syrian Archbishop of Jerusalem
> Anglican Bishop in Jerusalem and President Bishop of Anglican Church

The Greek-Catholic Patriarchal Vicar
The Lutheran Bishop of Jerusalem

Jerusalem, 20 December 1990

ϑℓϕ

Letter to the President of Iraq by the Heads of the Churches in Jerusalem and the Holy Land

On the occasion of the visit of the Secretary General of the United Nations to Baghdad in pursuit of a peaceful resolution of the current crisis, We, the Patriarchs and Heads of Christian Communities in Jerusalem and the Holy Land, on behalf of all peoples urge you to support all efforts of peace and to avoid war, to spare lives, and to promote a just resolution of all causes of conflict in the Middle East. A war never creates justice and peace, only suffering and more destruction.

Therefore, we extend this message of hope to your Excellencies, President George Bush and President Saddam Hussein, to consider most seriously this our plea, and the anxious cries of millions around the world.

We pray that you will decide for peace and relieve the current anxiety in the hearts of children, women, and men of all nations.

"Blessed are the peacemakers."

Jerusalem, January 12, 1991

ϑℓϕ

Urgent Appeal to the Leaders of the World by the Heads of the Christian Communities of the Holy Land

From Jerusalem, the City of Peace, we, the Heads of the Christian Communities of the Holy Land, address this urgent appeal to you.

We implore you to do everything possible to remove the threat of war in the region, and bring peace to this troubled spot on earth, so that future generations may live in peace and harmony together.

We urge you to concentrate all your efforts to salvage the peace of this region and avert the horror of war, which may erupt as a consequence of the escalating Gulf crisis.

We call upon you to "beat your swords into ploughshares and your spears into pruning forks" and to promulgate a spirit of international détente conducive to peace and understanding among all the nations of a world where conflicts are laid to rest and tensions are reduced.

We appeal to the world conscience to bestir itself, and pray to our Lord, the Light of the world, to inspire you with a new vision for a new world, where the wolf may indeed lie with the sheep.

We call on the international community to help pave the way for a new era of peace. We stand upon the threshold of the Third Millennium. Let us strive to make the moving force of the coming era fear of the Lord and love of our fellow beings, for there can be no power stronger than love. In all our undertakings, we shall be guided and sustained by the strength of the Holy Spirit.

We call upon believers in the entire world to join us in prayer on Sunday, January 13. Let a cry issue forth from the Church in Jerusalem and in the Holy Land for justice and reconciliation and peace on earth and goodwill among men.

Jerusalem, 13 January 1991

Statement Release (fragment)

In light of this inhumane situation, the Greek Orthodox, Latin, and Armenian Patriarchs, as well as the Custos of the Holy Land, met together on January 30 at the Armenian Orthodox Patriarchate, and sent a joint telegram to the President of the State of Israel:

"We hope to bring to the attention of Your Excellency our profound concern in light of the current situation. As of today it has been almost two weeks that the entire civilian population of the West Bank of Jordan and of Gaza, numbering 1.5 million people, has been under the strictest possible total curfew.[40] This type of collective punishment affects the daily lives of thousands of women, children, and elderly people. The extended curfew has resulted in considerable suffering for the entire population and has deprived the people of all their vital services. It has prevented believers from carrying out their religious obligations in all the places of worship.

"We ask that Your Excellency intercede forthwith to have this unwarranted curfew lifted and to allow citizens to return to their normal lives during these critical and difficult times. May God protect us all from the evils of war."

30 January 1991

EASTER MESSAGE of the PATRIARCHS and the HEADS of the CHURCHES of the HOLY LAND

As we celebrate the Resurrection of our Lord, we, the Patriarchs and the Heads of the Christian Churches in the Holy Land, share with you, our beloved Children, the message of joy and hope in the Risen Christ.

We have gathered to reflect on the events of the last months and the future of our region.

We have repeatedly expressed our opposition against war, violence, and use of force as means to resolve conflicts and misunderstanding between nations. We were deeply pained to witness a destructive war which took its heavy toll on human lives.

During the whole duration of the war, the Occupied Territories were subjected to an unwarranted harsh curfew causing considerable economic stress and human hardship. As a result, the population of the West Bank and Gaza are now in dire need of massive international financial support.

To date, despite local and international protest, it is more than forty months that Universities in the West Bank and Gaza remain closed. This has adversely affected the education of our youth, depriving them of one of their basic human rights. We call upon the Israeli authorities to honor their undertaking for free and unrestricted education.

The Christian churches of the Holy Land, throughout their long historical presence, and despite many vicissitudes, have managed to retain their historical rights in the service of their Faithful and the Holy Places. Today the churches face many difficulties in maintaining these rights. We stress again that our Historical Rights are not negotiable. The ongoing occupation of St. John's Hospice (adjoining the Holy Sepulchre) by Jewish settlers is a primary source of our concern. In this occupation we see an attempt to change the unique and pluralistic character of Jerusalem. We demand the authorities to honor their commitments towards the churches.

We are confident that the International Community, after the Gulf Crisis and war, is able to find a just solution for the Palestinian-Israeli conflict. A just solution would end the cycle of violence and injustice.

During this Holy Week we call upon you, Dear Faithful, and upon the whole world to pray fervently for the just solution of the Palestinian, Lebanese, and Cypriot problems. Let us pray for the recovery of peace, prosperity, and stability in our Holy Land.

Lasting peace is only possible through coexistence, reconciliation, and the fulfillment of the aspirations of all peoples by the attainment of their full Sovereignty.

May the risen Christ, who reconciled God with man through his Crucifixion, grant us, in this Holy Week, wisdom, strength, and inspiration for the reconciliation of all men, as children of the same Heavenly Father and Creator of the Universe.

We ask you, Dear Faithful, to pray in this spirit, especially during this Holy Week. May the Resurrected Christ bestow His blessings upon our Land and grant us lasting and just peace.

Greek Orthodox Patriarch of Jerusalem
Latin Patriarch of Jerusalem
Armenian Patriarch of Jerusalem
Custos of the Holy Land
Coptic Archbishop of Jerusalem
Syrian Archbishop of Jerusalem
Anglican Bishop in Jerusalem and Presiding Bishop of Anglican
   Church in the Middle East
The Greek-Catholic Patriarchal Vicar
The Lutheran Bishop of Jerusalem

Jerusalem, 23 March 1991

Statement Release (fragment)

In a joint declaration made on May 30, 1991, the Heads of the Church expressed "their profound concern and worry at the growing feeling of insecurity and fear among the people and within the Churches." They denounced the dissemination of biased news reports and anti-Christian demonstrations, and once again brought up the occupation of the Greek Orthodox Patriarchate's Saint John's Hospice, which they described as a "serious impingement on the historical rights of Christians, unprecedented in the history of the Holy City." They proceeded to call upon the authorities to "honor the historical inviolability and integrity" of the holy sites, the churches, and the convents and ended with the following wish: "May Almighty God inspire within all the leaders engaged in this conflict the desire to work towards peace and justice and to guide their people by using whatever channels are available, including the media, towards peace, reconciliation and the elimination of the underlying causes of social and political injustice and turmoil."

30 May 1991

MESSAGE to the DELEGATES of the PEACE CONFERENCE in MADRID from the PATRIARCHS and the HEADS of CHRISTIAN COMMUNITIES in JERUSALEM

"Blessed are the peace-makers, for they shall be called children of God."
    The churches in Jerusalem greet you in the name of the God of peace. From this Holy City we raise our prayers for all those who have worked tirelessly so that a new foundation for peace can be built. We pray as you begin your deliberations in Madrid that the Spirit of reconciliation and understanding will prevail and that justice and peace will come to our tormented land.
    We all face the challenge to be peacemakers. We repeat our deep commitment and pastoral concern for the welfare of all peoples in this land. As Patriarchs and Heads of the Christian Communities in Jerusalem with a continuous presence of two millennia in the Holy Land, and being entrusted

by the Universal Church to safeguard the Holy Places of Christianity, we call upon all parties concerned to remember that all people carry the same image and likeness of God and are children of the same Lord. We call upon you to persevere in your deliberations for the peoples of the Middle East.

We assure you of our constant prayers. On this very day as you meet in Madrid, thousands of Christians in the Holy Land, as well as throughout the world, are praying fervently for the success of the Peace Conference. We pray that you will be guided to lay the foundation for a peaceful resolution of the Middle East conflict based on justice and truth for all. We pray that all the people and countries of our region will be able to live in security, freedom, and dignity. We pray that the human and political rights of all will be guarded and democratic principles honored.

May the God of justice and peace guide you in all endeavors.

Jerusalem, 30 October 1991

Signed:

Greek Orthodox Patriarch of Jerusalem
H.B. Patriarch Diodoros

Latin Patriarch of Jerusalem
H.B. Michel Sabbah

Armenian Patriarch of Jerusalem
Archbishop Torkom Manougian

Custos of the Holy Land
Most Rev. Father Cechitelli (O.F.M.)

Coptic Archbishop of Jerusalem
H.B. Basilios

Syrian Archbishop of Jerusalem
Archbishop Dionysios Behnam Jijjawi

Anglican President Bishop in Jerusalem and the Middle East
Bishop Samir Kafity

Greek Catholic Patriarchal Vicar
Archbishop Lutfi Laham

Lutheran Bishop of Jerusalem
Bishop Naim Nassar

꧁꧂

STATEMENT from JERUSALEM HEADS of CHURCHES on PROTECTION of CHRISTIAN HOLY PLACES

As we have repeatedly stated in the past, we categorically condemn any attempt to modify the demographic and unique character and status of Jerusalem.

Collective punishment continues to be visited indiscriminately on the civilian Palestinian population. For a whole fortnight, from 1 December 1991 to 15 December 1991, total curfew was imposed on the Ramallah area and new restrictions placed on West Bank towns and the Gaza Strip, aggravating the severe restrictions of movement already in force since the beginning of last year. These measures, in addition to causing considerable hardship to people, have severely limited their freedom of access to the Holy Places in Jerusalem during Feast days.

We condemn the stabbing of the Patriarchal Vicar of the Syrian Catholic Church on Christmas Eve, and the assault on his convent.

We regret that the authorities who were alerted to the threat on his life did not take preventive measures and furthermore set the assailant free, before the settlement of the issue.

Around the dawn of the New Year, vandals slashed the tires of several cars belonging to Christian institutions, Consular missions, and Armenian residents parked near the Armenian Patriarchate and daubed racist slogans on a gate.

During the weekend of 28 December, a rare 6th century Byzantine mosaic was vandalized. The dedicatory Greek inscription of the apse was irreversibly damaged. Two funerary chambers belonging to an Armenian 6th century monastery were buried beneath a huge pile of rocks.

Several Christian vestiges, such as St. Stephen's monastic complex (near Damascus Gate) and St. George's monastery outside Jaffa Gate, have been denied posterity and buried under new highways.

We demand the authorities to provide protection against these depredations and take prompt action to forestall any further harassment in the future, and preserve the newly discovered relics of the Early Christian Church in Jerusalem. If no appropriate and satisfactory measures are taken to protect Christian archaeological sites, we will consider seeking international protection to preserve our universal Christian heritage.

We pray to the Almighty that peace and understanding may reign in our region and that His Holy Land may be blessed with stability and prosperity.

We call upon all the faithful to pray that the Lord may bestow upon us the grace of peace in the coming year.

Signed:
Greek Orthodox Patriarch of Jerusalem
Latin Patriarch of Jerusalem
Armenian Patriarch of Jerusalem
Custos of the Holy Land
Coptic Archbishop of Jerusalem
Syrian Archbishop of Jerusalem
Anglican Bishop in Jerusalem and Presiding Bishop of Anglican
    Church
Greek-Catholic Patriarchal Vicar
Lutheran Bishop of Jerusalem

STATEMENT by the PATRIARCHS and HEADS of the CHRISTIAN COMMUNITIES of JERUSALEM

Today, the Church of Jerusalem is in mourning.

A new act of desecration was committed on Calvary, in the Church of the Holy Sepulchre, the holiest shrine of Christianity.

The Tabernacle holding the Holy Sacrament has been smashed.

The Holy Cross of Calvary standing there for centuries has been uprooted.

The sacred objects of the two altars of Calvary have been thrown on the ground and shattered.

The glass case of the Madonna has been damaged.

The same Madonna on Calvary, about two months ago, was subjected to an indescribable indignity and robbery.

Shocked and outraged by this latest abomination of desecration, we met on Saturday night, the 2nd of May, 1992, to express our horror and indignation and to condemn this appalling act of vandalism, unparalleled in the recent history of the Church of Jerusalem.

Today, we met on Holy Calvary to ask God for forgiveness, and to ask him to console and protect His Church.

We have been witness to the Lord in the birthplace of Christianity for the last two thousand years. We stand firm in our faith and determination to safeguard the Holy Places, and we will continue to do so for the ultimate glory of God, against all odds.

We, the Guardians of the Holy Places, together with the members of our churches, are gathered here today at this Holy Shrine to ask all believers of the world to join us in prayer and acts of reparation at this moment of reconsecration.

May the Lord have mercy on us.

Monday, 4 May 1992

✐

STATEMENT by the PATRIARCHS and HEADS of the CHRISTIAN COMMUNITIES of the HOLY LAND issued on CHRISTMAS EVE

We, the Patriarchs and the Heads of Christian Communities in the Holy Land, entrusted with the spiritual guidance of our communities and actively participating in the life of the people of this country, and out of concern for the continuation of the peace process ardently desired by all people in this land, stated the following:

Recently there have been increasing signs of violence, and they are affecting the daily life of all inhabitants of this land.

We consider the mass deportation of Palestinians as an unacceptable form of collective punishment, and we hope the authorities will find a way so that they will return to their loved ones.

We call upon all people to contribute towards the dialogue for peace, so that love and compassion may prevail in the Holy Land.

We also urge our faithful to continue to preserve our places of worship as a haven of serenity and prayer.

We ask our congregations to pray for coexistence and reconciliation between all the people of the Holy Land.

TWO

The Oslo Years

- -

No Firm Foundation (1993-1996)

Jerusalem the Cornerstone

The Heads of Churches were silent from Christmas 1992 until November 1994.[1] These were years during which hope was tangled with a downward-spiraling situation on the ground. Israel took advantage of the Gulf War's diversion of the world's attention and increased expulsions of Palestinians. According to Sara Roy, when the far-right Moledet party, "which openly advocates expelling all Palestinians from the Occupied Territories," joined the Israeli government at the time the Gulf War broke out, Palestinian fears of mass deportation or transfer were heightened.[2] This fear, together with economic hardship and the brutality of the Israeli Defense Force, contributed to the Intifada's faltering nonviolent strategy. Slowly it shifted from a populist uprising by a whole people into a struggle waged by well-armed cadres.

The "peace process," nonetheless, continued in 1992, as talks in Madrid morphed into back-channel talks in Oslo, and led to the Oslo Accords. On 13 September 1993, the Declaration of Principles was signed on the White House lawn by Arafat and Rabin, with Bill Clinton as witness. Included in these Principles, was a clause that foretold the failure of the Oslo Accords. Article V:3 stated, "It is understood that those negotiations shall cover remaining issues, including Jerusalem, refugees, settlements, security arrangements, borders, relations, and cooperation with other neighbors and other issues of common interest."[3] Foremost among these so-called Permanent Status Issues was the status of Jerusalem for Israel and for Palestinians. In the context of this peace process, with its anticipation of future negotiation, the Jerusalem Heads of Churches began to prepare a statement titled "The Significance of Jerusalem for Christians." The statement, published on 14 November 1994, declared the following:

> Jerusalem is a city holy for the people of the three monotheistic religions: Judaism, Christianity, and Islam. Its unique nature of sanctity endows it with a special vocation: calling for reconciliation and harmony among people, whether citizens, pilgrims, or visitors. And because of its symbolic and emotive value, Jerusalem has been a rallying cry for different revived nationalistic and fundamentalist stirrings in the region and elsewhere. And, unfortunately, the city has become a source of conflict and disharmony. It is at the heart of the Israeli-Palestinian and Israeli-Arab disputes. While the mystical call of the city attracts believers, its present unenviable situation scandalizes many. The current Arab-Israeli peace process is on its way towards resolution of the Middle East conflict. Some new facts have already been established, some concrete signs posted. But in the process Jerusalem has again been side-stepped, because its status, and especially sovereignty over the city, are the most difficult questions to resolve in future negotiations. Nevertheless, one must already begin to reflect on the questions and do whatever is necessary to be able to approach them in the most favorable conditions when the moment arrives.

By this statement, the Jerusalem Heads of Churches confirmed they themselves would "do whatever is necessary" to ensure "the most favorable conditions" for future negotiations on the status and sovereignty of the city. The Jerusalem Heads of Churches also very intentionally, and astutely, issued a joint statement to make it clear to the Israeli government that it could not deal with the Jerusalem Heads of Churches individually, thereby attempting to divide the Heads of Churches on this foremost Permanent Status Issue: the status and sovereignty of Jerusalem.

The statement, signed by the nine churches named above, and also by the Coptic Orthodox and the Ethiopian Orthodox Archbishops and by the Maronite Patriarch Vicar, makes three particularly significant points. First, as noted above, the statement clearly recognizes the city as a holy city for Jews, Christians, and Muslims, and thereby affirms the city's "special vocation: calling for reconciliation and harmony among people." Second, the statement, accordingly, affirms that "all ought to enjoy full freedom of access to its Holy Places, and freedom of worship," and calls for the rights encoded in "the Status Quo of the Holy Places according to historical 'firmans' and other documents, . . . to be recognized and respected,"[4] and thereby to confirm the freedom of access for all religious communities as well as individuals.[5] Third, on the basis of these affirmations, the statement calls for a "special statute for Jerusalem" that "reflects the universal importance and significance of the city," a statute crafted by representatives of the three local faith communities and guaranteed by the international community.[6] The statement on the status and sovereignty of Jerusalem ends with a call to "all parties concerned to comprehend and accept the nature and deep significance of Jerusalem, City of God, . . . in order to give back to Jerusalem its true universal character and to make the city a holy place of reconciliation for humankind."

Escalation of Violence

But, on 30 March 1993, even before the first Oslo signing in September or the signing of the Fundamental Agreement in December 1993, Israel implemented a new policy regarding Jerusalem and the Occupied Territories: closure.[7] Jerusalem was closed to Palestinian inhabitants of the Occupied Territories. Checkpoints were erected.[8] Only Palestinians who had the Jerusalem identity cards[9] issued to permanent residents or who were issued special permits were allowed to enter the city. The application procedure for non-Jerusalemites to obtain a special permit continues to be complicated and drawn-out; it is intended to intimidate and discourage any application at all. This closure policy has separated families by making it impossible for Jerusalemites to obtain permission for spouses who are residents of another place. It has increased unemployment in the Territories because workers cannot obtain work permits to enter Jerusalem. The closure has also restricted access to hospitals and schools, and to the Holy Places.[10] Underlying this policy of closure regarding Jerusalem was another goal: separation from Palestinians. At this point, separation was enacted by the closure and confirmed by the building of settlements and a system of Israeli "ring roads."

The closure of Jerusalem was one sign of a worsening of the situation addressed by the Jerusalem Heads of Churches in their 1995 Easter Message. Along with the closure, there was an attempt to annex more of East Jerusalem; more and more land was expropriated. The building of settlements — old and new — continued at an ever increased pace.[11] Indeed, according to Ideith Zertal and Akiva Eldar, "the fall of 1994 to the fall of 1995 was a bitter year for the Oslo agreement and for anyone who believed in the possibility of making peace between Israel and the Palestinians. . . ."[12] Already in February 1994, an escalation of violence had begun when, on the day of Purim, a day to mark the deliverance of the Jewish people from extinction, Baruch Goldstein, a physician from Brooklyn then living in the settlement of Kiryat Arba, entered the Tomb of the Patriarchs in the nearby town of Hebron, pulled out an assault rifle, and fired 111 shots, killing more than twenty-nine worshipers and wounding one hundred and twenty-five. The Hebron massacre, and a sense that Oslo served Israeli interests alone, led to the first suicide attacks, instigated by Hamas[13] on 6 April 1994. This in turn led to further punitive measures, and then further Palestinian reprisals, and so on. Extremists — Israeli and Palestinian alike — lashed out against the Oslo Accords. This escalating cycle of violence came to a crescendo when Prime Minister Rabin, Israeli signer of the Accords, was assassinated by a zealot Jewish settler in November 1995. Benjamin Netanyahu's election was an anti-Oslo election. Thereafter, the building of settlements increased and house demolition began again, both measures brutally reinforcing the occupation.

Two months earlier, on 28 September 1995, the Oslo II agreement had been signed.[14] Once again, Rabin had held back from any explicit commitment to a suspension of settlement expansion. The agreement did, however, specify that "neither side shall initiate or take any step that will change the status of the West Bank and Gaza Strip pending the outcome of the permanent status negotiations."[15] This stipulation on paper did not then, or since, accord with "facts on the ground."

A year later, in September 1996, at the urging of then Jerusalem mayor and later Israeli Prime Minister Ehud Olmert, but against the counsel of all his advisors, Prime Minister Netanyahu, newly elected on a platform to end any "two-state solution" negotiation, gave the go-ahead to open the "Western Wall Tunnel," an archaeological tunnel that runs underneath the Haram al-Sharif.[16] The act provoked demonstrations and riots. Estimates of the numbers of Palestinians killed range from seventy-five to eighty-five; many more were injured. The tunnel, particularly in the eyes of Muslims, threatened the very foundation of the al-Aqsa Mosque and destroyed artifacts from various Muslim historical eras. More than this, for many Palestinians, the opening of the tunnel was a violation of the very "soul of Palestine."[17] As the Jerusalem Heads of Churches put it in their 29 September 1996 statement, the opening of the tunnel was "the straw that broke the camel's back."[18]

"Violence Can Never Lead to Peace"

A few months later, in November-December 1996, the Israeli army was re-deployed to Jenin, Nablus, Bethlehem, and Ramallah.[20] During these months, and earlier in 1996, the Heads of Churches issued statements to condemn acts of violence on all sides and to offer condolences to all be-reaved families. The 5 March 1996 statement is especially clear:

> Human life is a sacred gift from God, who created all men and women in his very own image, and no one has the right to desecrate it. We state unequivocally our belief that violence can never lead to peace, whether it comes from groups or states. Palestinians and Israelis must not allow violence and extremism to deter their quest and efforts for peace at this critical moment in our history.

And their 1996 Easter Message affirmed that this holy season is a time of "liberation and resurrection" when we celebrate the "triumph of life over death, of peace over violence," and so call for a new regard for all human beings.

Perhaps the most powerful — indeed, poignant — statement from this period is the 29 September 1996 statement, published after an ecumen-ical prayer service held by the Heads of Churches in Jerusalem at St. Anne's Church. The prayer service was called in the wake of the wave of riots fol-lowing the opening of the archaeological tunnel under al-Aqsa and al-Haram al-Sharif.[20] In the statement, the Heads of Churches confess that "we have been going through the way of the cross," and they declare,

> Our first response as Christians in the midst of crises is the response of prayer. We cry out to God to have mercy on all of us. . . . As we lift our voices in prayer, we wish to emphasize three principles that spring from

the core of our faith in God and grow out of experience of the Christian Church in this country for the past 2,000 years.

The three principles named are these. First, "Peace and security in our country cannot prevail unless they are established on justice." Second, "Our faith teaches us that there is no difference between the life of one person and another. There is no difference in God's eyes between Jew and Palestinian, between Arab and foreigner. God is the creator of all. As believers in one God, we plainly state that all must live under the same law," and here the Heads of Churches call the Israeli government to end discriminatory laws, "abstain from the confiscation of land, to return confiscated land . . . , to stop the demolition of homes, to release all prisoners and detainees, to remove roadblocks, and to respect all signed agreements." Third, it is critical to "close the recently opened tunnel, to refrain from causing insult and humiliation to the Palestinian people, and treat the Palestinians as genuine partners, who are seeking a life of freedom and dignity in their own country and on their own land." The statement concludes,

> "Jerusalem first" is now a priority. It is the heart of the conflict and the key to peace. When the closure of Jerusalem is lifted and the two parties share sovereignty over it, Jerusalem will become the city of peace. . . . a city that will be a model for the peaceful coexistence between two peoples . . . and a genuine symbol of authentic brotherhood and tolerance between the three faiths. . . . We call on all authorities concerned to end the violence, to work for the establishment of justice, so stability might be realized . . . and our Jerusalem will have the peace for which we all strive and pray.

A few months later, in their 1996 Christmas Message, the Heads of Churches are clear:

> [1996] . . . has not been a year of peace. . . . Instead, we have witnessed the harvest of hatred and enmity manifesting itself in the form of death and suffering. . . . Hope has turned to despair and goodwill to mistrust. Suicide bombings, wholesale closures, and rising extremism have impacted Jews, Christians, and Muslims alike. Hopes for peace have been stunted by human violence and unyielding postures. At such a critical period, we need to turn to the infant Jesus, born in a modest manger in

Bethlehem. We need to make room for the Savior child in our hearts if we want to overstep mistrust and mutual negation. If the child cannot be born in our hearts, then the child will not be born at all.

Events early in 1997 portended no better. The most explosive event was the expropriation of the hill Jabal Abu Ghneim[21] to build a new Israeli settlement, Har Homa. The building of this settlement completed the encirclement of Jerusalem by Jewish settlements, the encirclement intended to tip the demographic balance of so-called Greater Jerusalem in Israel's favor. According to Naseer H. Aruri, Har Homa also represented "an advanced stage in the Judaization of Bethlehem," making it "as vulnerable to the Etzion bloc of settlements as Hebron has been to Kiryat Arba."[22] These two projects, he argues, will split the West Bank "into two halves, a northern sector and a southern sector, both of which [will be] thoroughly atomized by Jewish settlements and by-pass roads exclusively for Jews."[23] Har Homa is located on land that belongs to Christians living in Beit Sahour and neighboring village Umm Tuba.

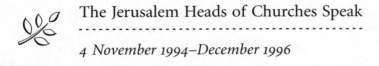

The Jerusalem Heads of Churches Speak

4 November 1994–December 1996

Jerusalem, 14th November 1994

Memorandum of Their Beatitudes the Patriarchs of the Heads of the Christian Communities in Jerusalem on the Significance of Jerusalem for Christians

1. Preamble
On the 14th of November 1994, the Heads of Christian Communities in Jerusalem met in solemn conclave to discuss the status of the Holy City and the situation of Christians living there, at the conclusion of which, they issued the following declaration:

2. Jerusalem, Holy City
Jerusalem is a city holy for the people of the three monotheistic religions: Judaism, Christianity, and Islam. Its unique nature of sanctity endows it with a special vocation: calling for reconciliation and harmony among people, whether citizens, pilgrims, or visitors. And because of its symbolic and emotive value, Jerusalem has been a rallying cry for different revived nationalistic and fundamentalist stirrings in the region and elsewhere. And, unfortunately, the city has become a source of conflict and disharmony. It is at the heart of the Israeli-Palestinian and Israeli-Arab disputes. While the mystic call of the city attracts believers, its present unenviable situation scandalizes many.

3. The Peace Process

The current Arab-Israeli peace process is on its way towards resolution of the Middle East conflict.[24] Some new facts have already been established, some concrete signs posted. But in the process Jerusalem has again been side-stepped, because its status, and especially sovereignty over the city, are the most difficult questions to resolve in future negotiations. Nevertheless, one must already begin to reflect on the questions and do whatever is necessary to be able to approach them in the most favorable conditions when the moment arrives.

4. Present Positions

When the different sides involved now speak of Jerusalem, they often assume exclusivist positions. Their claims are very divergent, indeed conflicting. The Israeli position is that Jerusalem should remain the unified and eternal capital of the State of Israel, under the absolute sovereignty of Israel alone. The Palestinians, on the other hand, insist that Jerusalem should become the capital of a future State of Palestine, although they do not lay claim to the entire modern city, but envisage only the Eastern, Arab part.

4. Lessons of History

Jerusalem has had a long, eventful history. It has known numerous wars and conquests, has been destroyed time and again, only to be reborn anew and rise from its ashes, like the mythical phoenix. Religious motivation has always gone hand in hand with political and cultural aspirations, and has often played a preponderant role. This motivation has often led to exclusivism or at least to the supremacy of one people over the others. But every exclusivity or every human supremacy is against the prophetic character of Jerusalem. Its universal vocation and appeal is to be a city of peace and harmony among all who dwell therein.

Jerusalem, like the entire Holy Land, has witnessed throughout its history the successive advent of numerous new peoples: they come from the desert, from the sea, from the north, from the east. Most often the newcomers were gradually integrated into the local population. This was a constant characteristic. But when the newcomers tried to claim exclusive possession of the city and the land, or refused to integrate themselves, then the others rejected them.

Indeed, the experience of history teaches us that in order for Jerusalem to be a city of peace, no longer lusted after from the outside and thus a bone of contention between warring sides, it cannot belong excessively to one people or to only one religion. Jerusalem should be open to all, shared by all. Those who govern the city should make it "the capital of humankind." This universal vision of Jerusalem would help those who exercise power there to open it to others who also are fondly attached to it and to accept sharing it with them.

6. The Christian Vision of Jerusalem

Through the prayful reading of the Bible, Christians recognize in faith that the long history of the people of God, with Jerusalem as it Center, is the history of salvation which fulfills God's design in and through Jesus of Nazareth, the Christ.

The one God has chosen Jerusalem to be the place where His name alone will dwell in the midst of His people so that they may offer to Him acceptable worship. The prophets look up to Jerusalem, especially after the purification of the exile: Jerusalem will be called "the city of justice, faith city" (Is. 1:26-27) where "the Lord dwells in holiness as in Sinai" (cf. Ps. 68:18). The Lord will place the city in the middle of the nations (Ex. 5:5), where the Second Temple will become a house of prayer for all peoples (Is. 2:2, 56:6-7). Jerusalem, aglow with the presence of God (Is. 60:1), ought to be a city whose gates are always open (Is. 17).

In the vision of their faith, Christians believe the Jerusalem of the Prophets to be the foreseen place of the salvation in and through Jesus Christ. In the Gospels, Jerusalem rejects the Sent-One, the Savior; and He weeps over it because this city of the Prophets that is also the city of the essential salvific events — the death and resurrection of Jesus — has completely lost sight of the path to peace (cf. Lk. 19:42).

In the Acts of the Apostles, Jerusalem is the place of the gift of the Spirit, of the birth of the Church; the community of the disciples of Jesus who are to be His witnesses not only in Jerusalem but even [to] the ends of the earth (1:8). In Jerusalem, the first Christian community incarnated the ecclesial ideal, and thus it remains a continuing reference point.

The Book of Revelation proclaims the anticipation of the new, heavenly Jerusalem (3:12; 21:2; cf. Gal. 4:26; Heb. 12:22). This holy city is the image of the new creation and the aspirations of all peoples, where God will wipe away all tears, and "there shall be no more death or mourning, crying out of pain, for the former world has passed away" (21:4).

7. The earthly Jerusalem, in the Christian tradition, prefigures the heavenly Jerusalem as "the vision of peace." In the Liturgy, the Church itself receives the name of Jerusalem and relives all of that city's anguish, joys, and hopes. Furthermore, during the first centuries the liturgy of Jerusalem became the foundation of all liturgies everywhere, and later deeply influenced the development of diverse liturgical traditions, because of the many pilgrimages to Jerusalem and of the symbolic meaning of the Holy City.

8. The pilgrimages slowly developed an understanding of the need to unify the sanctification of space through celebrations at the Holy Places with the sanctification in times through the calendared celebrations of the holy events of salvation (Egeria,[25] Cyril of Jerusalem[26]). Jerusalem soon occupied a unique place in the heart of Christianity everywhere. A theology and spirituality of pilgrimage developed. It was an ascetic time of biblical refreshment at the sources, a time of testing during which Christians recalled that they are strangers and pilgrims on earth (cf. Heb. 11:13) and that their personal and community vocation always and everywhere is to take up the cross and follow Jesus.

9. The Continuing Presence of a Christian Community

For Christianity, Jerusalem is the place of roots, ever living and nourishing. In Jerusalem is born every Christian. To be in Jerusalem is for every Christian to be at home.

For almost two thousand years, through so many hardships and the succession of so many powers, the local Church has been witnessing to the life and preaching the death and resurrection of Jesus Christ upon the same Holy Places, and its faithful have been receiving other brothers and sisters in the faith, as pilgrims, resident or in transit, inviting them to be re-immersed into the refreshing, ever living ecclesiastical sources. That continuing presence of a living Christian community is inseparable from the historical sites. Through the "living stones" the holy archaeological sites take on "life."

10. The City as Holy and as Other Cities

(1) a Holy City with holy places most precious to Christians because of their link with the history of salvation fulfilled in and through Jesus Christ;

(2) a city with a community of Christians which has been living continually there since its origins.

Thus for the local Christians, as well as for local Jews and Muslims, Jerusalem is not only a Holy City, but also their native city where they live, whence their right to continue to live there freely, with all the rights which obtain from that.

11. Legitimate Demands of Christians for Jerusalem

Insofar as Jerusalem is the quintessential Holy City, it above all ought to enjoy full freedom of access to its Holy Places, and freedom of worship. Those rights of property ownership, custody, and worship which the different churches have acquired throughout the history should continue to be retained by the same communities. These rights, which are already protected in the Status Quo of the Holy Places according to historical "firmans" and other documents, should continue to be recognized and respected.[27]

The Christians of the entire world, Western or Eastern, should have the right to come on pilgrimage to Jerusalem. They ought to be able to carry out their pilgrimage in the spirit of their authentic tradition: [free] to visit and to move around, to pray at holy sites, to embark into spiritual attendance and respectful practice of their faith, to enjoy the possibility of a prolonged stay and the benefits of hospitality and dignified lodgings.

12. The local Christian communities should enjoy all those rights to enable them to continue their active presence in freedom and to fulfill their responsibilities towards their own local members and towards the Christian pilgrims throughout the world.

Local Christians, not only in their capacity as Christians per se, but like all other citizens, religious or not, should enjoy the same fundamental rights for all: social, cultural, political, and national.

Among these rights are

- the human right of freedom of worship and of conscience, both as individuals and as religious communities,[28]
- civil and historical rights which allow them to carry out their religious, educational, medical, and other duties of charity,
- [and] the right to have their own institutions, such as hospices for pilgrims, institutions for the study of the Bible and the Traditions, centers for encounters with believers of other religions, monasteries, churches, cemeteries, and so forth and the right to have their own personnel man and run these institutions.

13. In claiming these rights for themselves, Christians recognize and respect similar and parallel rights of Jewish and Muslim believers and their communities. Christians declare themselves disposed to search with Jews and Muslims for a mutually respectful application of these rights and for a harmonious coexistence, in the perspective of the universal spiritual vocation of Jerusalem.

14. Special Statute for Jerusalem
All this presupposes a special judicial and political statute for Jerusalem which reflects the universal importance and significance of the city.

(1) In order to satisfy the national aspirations of all its inhabitants, and in order that Jews, Christians, and Muslims can be "at home" in Jerusalem and at peace with one another, representatives from the three monotheistic religions, in addition to local political powers, ought to be associated in the elaboration and application of such a special statute.

(2) Because of the universal significance of Jerusalem, the international community ought to be engaged in the stability and permanence of this statute. Jerusalem is too precious to be dependent solely on municipal or national political authorities, whoever they may be. Experience shows that an international guarantee is necessary.

Experience shows that such local authorities, for political reasons or the claims of security, sometimes are required to violate the rights of free access to the Holy Places. Therefore it is necessary to accord Jerusalem a special statute which will allow Jerusalem not to be victimized by laws imposed as a result of hostilities or wars but to be an open city which transcends local, regional, or world political troubles. This statute, established in common by local political and religious authorities, should also be guaranteed by the international community.

Conclusion
Jerusalem is a symbol and a promise of the presence of God, of fraternity and peace for humankind, in particular the children of Abraham: Jews, Christians, and Muslims.[29]

We call upon all parties concerned to comprehend and accept the nature and deep significance of Jerusalem, City of God. None can appropriate it in exclusivist ways. We invite each party to go beyond all exclusivist visions or actions, and without discrimination to consider the religious and national aspirations of others, in order to give back to Jerusalem its true universal character and to make of the city a holy place of reconciliation for humankind.

> H.B. Diordoros I — *Greek Orthodox Patriarch*
> H.G. Archbishop David Sahagin for the *Armenian Patriarch*
> H.G. Dr. Anba Abraham — *Coptic Archbishop*
> H.G. Abba Matheos — *Ethiopian Archbishop*
> Archbishop Lutfi Laham — *Greek Catholic Patriarchal Vicar*
> Mgr. Augustine Harfouche — *Maronite Patriarchal Vicar*
> H.B. Michel Sabbah — *Latin Patriarch*
> Very Rev. Fr. Joseph Nazzaro — *Custos of the Holy Land*
> H.G. Dionysios Jijjawi — *Syriac Archbishop*
> H.G. Bishop Samir Kafity — *Anglican Bishop*
> H.G. Bishop Naim Nassar — *Lutheran Bishop*
> Mgr. Pierre Abdel-Ahed — *Catholic-Syriac Patriarchal Vicar*

Jerusalem, 14 November 1994

Press Release by Jerusalem Heads of Churches

On 10 January 1995, the patriarchs and bishops of Jerusalem jointly delivered a letter to the Israeli Prime Minister Yitzhak Rabin, in his capacity as the Minister of Defense and Religious Affairs, in which they requested that he grant "free access to that part of the Jordan Bank that is considered one of the most sacred places . . . for all of Christianity," which would be especially apt coming on the heels of the establishment of diplomatic ties between Israel and Jordan. Furthermore, they added, "We next request the right to restore our monasteries, churches, and chapels situated in this region and to have continuous access to these, not only for the clergy, but also for the pilgrims and believers in our communities when they are accompanied by authorized clergy."[30]

On 23 January 1995, another statement declared, "We denounce this outrageous incident and unreservedly condemn all criminal actions that bring pain to innocent citizens and their families."

Statement Release (fragment)

We are all brothers gathered around the Tomb of the Resurrection to pray. Great is our suffering when we hear the echoes of fear, hatred, and violence around us, here in the very places where the voice of Christ once invoked mercy, peace, and love, love for God and for our fellowmen, whomsoever they may be. How is it possible for us to keep quiet when we see the city of the Most High, the city of redemption, a source of peace for the entire world, isolated, and its doors closed to its children?[31]

6 April 1995

Press Release from the Patriarchs and Heads of the Christian Churches in Jerusalem

We, the Patriarchs and Heads of the Christian Churches in Jerusalem, are appalled by the recent killings of innocent people, and we strongly condemn again all acts of violence, whatever their origin. We express our deepest sympathies and condolences to the bereaved families, our sincere wishes to the wounded, and our solidarity with all those who suffer.

Human life is a sacred gift from God, who created all men and women in his very own image, and no one has the right to desecrate it. We state unequivocally our belief that violence can never lead to peace, whether it comes from groups or states. Palestinians and Israelis must not allow violence and extremism to deter their quest and efforts for peace at this critical moment in our history.[32]

We believe that both the Palestinian and Israeli Authorities must cooperate together to create a new climate of peace in the area based on a full respect of the human person.

All the various Religious Authorities in the Land have a responsibility and a role in the creation and the facilitation of a new atmosphere of peace. This can only be done through meetings and dialogue between the leading Religious Authorities.

We address a fervent appeal to all in authority and to all political and religious parties to accept and to work for an honorable peace for both Israelis and Palestinians. Peace is the only guarantee for tranquility and security of all.

Jerusalem, March 5, 1996

Diodoros I
   Greek Orthodox Patriarch of Jerusalem
Michel Sabbah
   Latin Patriarch of Jerusalem
Torkom Manoogian
   Armenian Patriarch of Jerusalem
Fr. Giuseppe Nazzaro, O.F.M.
   Custos of the Holy Land
Anba Abraham
   Coptic Orthodox Bishop of Jerusalem
Fr. Shim'on Jan
   For the Syrian Orthodox Church
Abba Matheos
   Ethiopian Archbishop of Jerusalem
Samir Kaf'ity
   Anglican Bishop in Jerusalem
Lutfi Laham
   Greek Catholic Patriarchal Vicar
Naim Nassar
   Lutheran Bishop in Jerusalem
Andre Bedoglouian
   Armenian Catholic Patriarchal Vicar
Msgr. Boutros Abdel Ahad
   Syrian Catholic Patriarchal Vicar

Statement Release (fragment)

We are certain that land expropriations have always been and shall always be one of the principal causes of the sapping of a people's hopes, expectations, and sense of peace and security. They do not contribute towards establishing security among the inhabitants or the pursuit of peace.

We therefore call upon the Israeli authorities, who continue to affirm their decision to salvage the peace process that they began, to definitively stop the land expropriations in Bethlehem and in all Palestinian cities.[33]

29 March 1996

Patriarchs and Heads of Christian Churches in Jerusalem

Easter Message 1996

Dear brothers and sisters,

1. "Christ is risen!" (Lk. 24:1-52). Jesus, Lord and Savior, is risen, as he has foretold his apostles: "They will put him to death, and on the third day he will rise again" (Mt. 17:23). After the sufferings and the death of Our Lord Jesus Christ, we announce to you the glory of his Resurrection, with the hope and the strength which emanate from it. Before he, himself, took the cross, Jesus called his disciples to bear the cross and to follow him. He called his disciples to walk the narrow way which is the way to salvation.

2. This double vision of the cross and the resurrection applies to the situation which we are now experiencing: our sufferings are many, due to renewed times of violence and reprisals. As we sympathize with the families of the victims of extremism, we feel the pain of every home and every family deprived [of] jobs, exposed to painful daily life, due to the closure imposed as a reprisal. Even in this sequence of struggle between extremism and government and the peace process, and suffering which results from this struggle in our daily life, we see the way

57

of the cross, which will lead finally to the glory of the resurrection, when peace will prevail through hearts' reconciliation.

We understand that fighting extremism is not an easy task. We understand the responsibility of the governments to protect the innocent people from all extremism. But we understand, also, that in this task our governments should never indulge in the same logic of violence which they condemn as extremism. We ask them to find security measures which protect all, Palestinians and Israelis, without discrimination; in fact it is obvious that the present security measures are punishing only Palestinians. Moreover, some measures which implicate violence were imposed long before the last terrorist attacks and are still exercised as the confiscation of lands and the closure of Jerusalem.

Palestinians and Israelis alike ask for peace. But as the Prophet says: "They say, 'Peace, peace,' whereas there is no peace" (Jer. 6:14).

3. We celebrate in these days the paschal festivities. The experience of Easter and of Pesach is one of liberation and reconciliation. We invite our Authorities to live the experience of liberation and resurrection, which means the triumph of life over death, of peace over violence. We invite them, in the light of Pesach and Easter, to have a new look at the human beings, at the security measures, at the confiscation of lands, and at all kinds of decisions, so that every action will support peace and oppose violence.

Looking at the One God who manifested his power over servitude and over death, something new should appear in the hearts and in the actions of those leaders who have so far manifested their goodwill to build a new society.

4. We live in historical moments and in a difficult birth of a new era for Jerusalem, for Palestinians, and for the entire region. We ask our faithful and all believers to share in making peace and to stand against all forms of violence with their prayers, and with renewed and constructive hope and strength, through their faith in the Risen Lord.

5. We address our appeal to the Palestinian People, Christians and Muslims, and invite them to allow peace to be born and to cease all violence. We address the same appeal also to the Jewish people. Palestinians are your peace partners, your brothers for building a new Israeli and Palestinian society. They are no more enemies to be sacrificed for any manifestation of violence, for public opinion, or for an electoral campaign. "Do not oppress the weak," says the Lord (Amos 4:1).

6. We call again for an encounter and dialogue between the religious leaders of all faiths in this land, in order to plan how to re-educate our peoples according to the principles of mutual recognition, understanding, equality, and brotherhood. Each one should no longer see in the other an enemy but a brother and a sister with whom to build a new society and the new era in the region. This dialogue is necessary in order to support the peace process and make it possible.

7. We appeal to our Authorities to open the doors of the Holy City of Jerusalem, as we call upon our faithful to come and share with us the spiritual and enriching experience of the Holy Week and Easter in Jerusalem.

   Our message for all is a message of hope, of compassion, of reconciliation and joy. To all our priests and faithful, we say: In this blessed Easter time, be of one heart, one voice before the Lord, so that all of us "may come to know him and the power of his resurrection" (Phil. 3:10), in a true and definitive peace.

Jerusalem, Easter 1996

+ Diodoros I, Greek Orthodox Patriarch of Jerusalem
+ Michel Sabbah, Latin Patriarch of Jerusalem
+ Torkom Manooghian, Armenian Patriarch of Jerusalem
  Fr. Giuseppe Nazzaro, O.F.M., Custos of the Holy Land
+ Anba Abraham, Coptic Orthodox Bishop of Jerusalem
  P. Shim'on Jan, for the Syrian Orthodox Church
+ Abba Matheos, Ethiopian Archbishop of Jerusalem
+ Samir Kafity, Anglican Bishop in Jerusalem
+ Lutfi Laham, Greek Catholic Patriarchal Vicar
+ Naim Nassar, Lutheran Bishop in Jerusalem
+ Andre Bedoglouian, Armenian Catholic Patriarchal Vicar
  Msgr. Boutros Abdel Ahad, Syrian Catholic Patriarchal Vicar

April 1996

CALL for PEACE and JUSTICE in the HOLY LAND

"The effect of justice will be peace and the result of justice, quietness and security forever." (Isaiah 32:17)

A STATEMENT OF THE PATRIARCHS, BISHOPS, CLERGY, AND PEOPLE OF THE CHRISTIAN CHURCHES OF JERUSALEM. They are The Greek Orthodox Patriarch, The Latin Patriarch, The Armenian Patriarch, The Custos of the Holy Land, Coptic Archbishop, Syriac Archbishop, Ethiopian Archbishop, Anglican Bishop, Greek Catholic Patriarchal Vicar, Maronite Patriarchal Vicar, Lutheran Bishop, and Catholic Syriac Patriarchal Vicar.

September 29, 1996

Our Dear Brothers and Sisters,

For the past few days we have been going through the way of the cross. Together we have experienced feelings of pain and bitterness as we lived through the events that have shaken Jerusalem and the whole of our country, events that have led to the death of scores of people and [the] wounding of hundreds.[34]

Our first response as Christians in the midst of crises is the response of prayer. We cry out to God to have mercy on all of us, and to grant wisdom to the leaders of all the peoples of this land so that they might make the right decisions that will put an end to bloodshed and lead us to a just peace.

As we lift our voices in prayer, we wish to emphasize three principles that spring from the core of our faith in God and grow out of experience of the Christian Church in this country for the past 2,000 years.

1. Peace and security in our country cannot prevail unless they are established on justice. We believe that God is the God of justice and righteousness. God does not accept oppression, but calls on all of us as members of one human family, Arabs and Jews, to make justice and to love righteousness. God does not accept the domination of the powerful or their arrogance. Our faith assures us that any effort by the governing authority to impose peace in our country, which is not established on justice and righteousness, will lead to failure and disaster. We, therefore, urgently call on the Israeli government to pursue the peace process with all seriousness and to carry out all its obligations to our people. We urge the Israeli

government to change its attitude and purify its motives. Peace cannot be imposed by the power of arms. Brutality will not lead to security. Stability cannot be established by way of injustice and the denial of rights. Justice must come first, and then peace will follow; a peace that will lead to security. We as Christians feel that the Israeli government's formula for peace is flawed. Its slogan is "security first and then peace." Such a formula casts justice aside and will never bring peace. As the prophet Isaiah has said, "The effect of justice will be peace and the result of justice, quietness and security forever" (Isaiah 32:17).

2. Our faith teaches us that there is no difference between the life of one person and another. There is no difference in God's eyes between Jew and Palestinian, between Arab and foreigner. God is the creator of all. As believers in one God, we plainly state that all must live under the same law. We, therefore, call on the Israeli government to bring all its discriminatory policies to an end. Palestinians should have rights in their country, just as Jews have rights in their country. This is the only way that peace can prevail. Every time the Israeli government gives preferential treatment to the Jews over Palestinians, it sows the seed of hatred and violence and thus is responsible for the growth of animosity towards its own people. We urge the Israeli government to abstain from the confiscation of land, to return confiscated land to its rightful owners, to stop the demolition of homes, to release all prisoners and detainees, to remove roadblocks, and to respect all signed agreements. We call upon the Israeli government to close the recently opened tunnel, to refrain from causing insult and humiliation to the Palestinian people, and [to] treat the Palestinians as genuine partners, who are seeking a life of freedom and dignity in their own country and on their own land. Racial discrimination does not lead to peace and security. Discrimination cannot be the basis for building trust between the two peoples.

3. The opening of the tunnel in the Old City of Jerusalem was only the straw that broke the camel's back. However, the opening of the tunnel itself has great significance, for it has touched the religious nerve of our Muslim brothers and sisters. The religious nerve in our country is the most sensitive nerve of all. A just and democratic government does not violate the religious sensitivity of others in this way. The easiest fire to kindle is the fire of religious opening of other tunnels, which will inevitably lead to breaking into [the] compound of the Mosque and the occupation of a part of it. Further archaeological claims near the tunnel might also affect Christian sites and restrict pilgrims in the area. Therefore, what is required is the

closure of the tunnel, along with [a] pledge to the Muslim community that Israeli violation of Muslim or Christian holy places [will stop].

"Jerusalem first" is now a priority. It is the heart of the conflict and the key to peace. When the closure of Jerusalem is lifted and the two parties share sovereignty over it, Jerusalem will become the city of peace. If Israel maintains an exclusive sovereignty over the city, and continues its "judaization," Jerusalem will never be the city of peace. Any peace imposed by the iron fist will remain a fake and temporary peace. Jews will never feel secure and Palestinians will never submit to it. We therefore insist on an open Jerusalem, the capital for two states, a city that will be a model for the peaceful coexistence between two peoples, Palestinian and Israeli. Thus, Jerusalem will become a genuine symbol of authentic brotherhood and tolerance between the three faiths: Islam, Judaism, and Christianity.

We call on all authorities concerned to end the violence to work for the establishment of justice, so that stability might be realized. We ask God to fill our hearts and minds with love, strength, and all that is good, so that our region, our country, and our Jerusalem will have the peace for which we all strive and pray.

Patriarchs and Heads of Christian Communities in Jerusalem

Christmas Message 1996

Beloved Brothers and Sisters in Christ,

As we welcome the dawning of a new Christmas, we are reminded of how the angels sang, "Glory to God in the highest and peace to God's people on Earth" (Luke 2:14).

1996, however, has not been a year of peace for people in the Holy Land. Instead, we have witnessed the harvest of hatred and enmity manifesting itself in the form of death and suffering amongst all the children of our forefather Abraham. Hope has turned to despair and goodwill to mistrust. Suicide bombings, wholesale closures, and rising extremism have impacted Jews, Christians, and Muslims alike. Hopes for peace have been stunted by human violence and unyielding postures.

At such a critical period, we need to turn again to the infant Jesus, born in a modest manger in Bethlehem. We need to make room for the Savior child in our hearts if we want to overstep mistrust and mutual negation. If the child cannot be born in our hearts, then the child will not be born at all. Are we willing to transform our hearts into cribs that are ready to receive God and facilitate his presence within us? Are we ready to implement Christ's command to love one another — a command as relevant to our world, which stands on the threshold of the new millennium, as it was 2,000 years ago?

At this time of uncertain peace, the Christian community is called to nurture Christ's presence in this land. We must be the crib that embraces and protects the Prince of Peace, that represents the message of love and hope to the whole community and to all peoples. We must prepare Him room so that we might be His hands and feet, taking the initiative for peace. We need to teach ourselves how to go beyond our own human restrictions and limitations as well as those we impose upon others. The Christmas message leads us to seek a place where there is openness, room for common growth and new beginnings.

As we look to a new year, we also pray for renewed hope amongst the two peoples of this land. Let all governments respect the dignity and human rights of everyone. Let all people respect others as they respect themselves and, as called for by the prophet Amos, "Let justice roll down like waters, and righteousness like an ever-flowing stream"(5:24).

As Children of God, we all have a duty to pray and work for peace and to suffer with those whose lives are dimmed by the darkness of oppression. We cherish all efforts toward peace in the Holy Land. We wish God's wisdom and guidance to all the political leaders; may they have the strength and enjoy success so that our region will be blessed with the fruits of their mutual efforts — the joy of real peace. That should be our Christmas gift to each other and the real fruit of the Christmas season.

We pray that our Savior the Christ child, who has power over all evil, fills you with His blessings. May He bless you in the name of the Father, the Son, and the Holy Spirit, One God forever and ever. Amen.

Jerusalem, Christmas 1996

THREE Intifada II

The Way of the Cross (1998-2002)

Churches under Siege

A late November 1998 statement was sent to the Israeli President and
Prime Minister, challenging the escalated withdrawal of residence cards
from Jerusalem Palestinians.[1] By April 1999, the attention of the Heads of
Churches in Jerusalem was riveted by the tense situation in Nazareth. On
4 April, a group of Islamists occupied the long-vacated buildings of an old
school directly in front of the Basilica of the Annunciation, with the intention of establishing a mosque only a few meters away from the basilica.
This was particularly provocative because these were months of intense
preparation in Nazareth, as well as in Bethlehem and Jerusalem, for the
celebration of the second millennium. Churches also refer to other "very
serious incidents" in Nazareth, including the desecration of Christian
symbols. The 5 April statement specifies, "An atmosphere of fear has been
created." Magnifying the Christian community's sense of being besieged
was the absence of any response by the Israeli government. The Jerusalem
Heads of Churches therefore ". . . urge the Government of Israel to bear its
responsibilities and to take the appropriate means to stop the violence and
to restore order and security for all and to preserve the sacredness of the
City of the Annunciation."

Once again, the Heads of Churches not only published a statement;
once again, they took action. They decided to close all churches in Nazareth,
including the basilica, except for liturgical offices, on 6-7 April. This closure

was extended to "all the Sanctuaries of the Holy Land" on 22-23 November 1999, after an Israeli ministry gave "the go-ahead for the laying of the cornerstone to this construction [of the mosque] on 8 November 1999," a decision that was "maintained despite numerous and repeated interventions by different ecclesiastical and secular bodies." Churches besieged.

Signs of Hope

After the November 1999 closure of Christian holy places, two signs of hope appeared, one religious and one political, insofar as that distinction makes any sense in this land called holy. In Bethlehem, on 4 December 1999, close to five thousand people gathered — local and international, lay and clergy and religious, hierarchs and pilgrims — to sing hymns and pray for peace, to hear the reading of scripture and messages of greeting and support, and to be heartened by choirs' anthems. "It was probably the most beautiful and meaningful ecumenical manifestation the Churches in Jerusalem have witnessed in modern history," reported Father Frans Bouwen in *Proche-Orient Chrétien.* "In the common message they published on this occasion, the Heads of Churches confessed that they had not been faithful to Jesus' prayer for the unity of his disciples and renewed their commitment to work for unity and for common witness, in the service of peace, in the interreligious context of the Holy Land."[2]

After the service in Manger Square, the Jerusalem Heads of Churches together entered the Church of the Nativity; this joint entry was unprecedented, and powerfully signified an ecumenical advance beyond Status Quo legislation of access and use of the Holy Places in Bethlehem and Jerusalem and on the Mount of Olives.

A second sign of hope was the Camp David meeting in July 2000. Just before the meeting, the Heads of Churches sent a letter to Prime Minister Ehud Barak and to President Yasser Arafat (15 July 2000) and another to Barak, Arafat, and Clinton (21 July 2000). The second of these letters "lifts up the hopes of the two peoples and three religions of this land — Palestinians and Israelis, Jews, Christians, and Muslims alike." This formula — the two peoples and three religions of this land — appeared only very occasionally in prior communications; from here onward it is often repeated.

The letter to Barak, Arafat, and Clinton also calls, once again, for the leaders to honor the "special privileges that were codified by the 'Status

Quo' provisions as much as by custom and tradition over many centuries." Reference is made to the 14 November 1994 statement on the status and significance of Jerusalem for Christians to ask that any agreement guarantee that "the fundamental freedoms of worship and access by all Christians to their Holy Sanctuaries and to their headquarters within the Old City are not impeded in any way whatsoever," ensuring "a quality of right of access" by "a system of international guarantees."

"Father, forgive them . . ."

On 28 September 2000, Ariel Sharon made his infamous foray onto Al-Haram al-Sharif, the Temple Mount. Immediately after Sharon's departure, demonstrators rioted, and riots spread throughout East Jerusalem. The next day, during Friday midday prayers at the Al-Aqsa Mosque, there were violent disturbances, followed by a hasty police response. Seven Palestinians were killed; more than one hundred were wounded. Once again, blood was shed on this holy site, again as Muslims gathered there for midday prayers.

It has often been said that this incident provoked the second, so-called Al-Aqsa Intifada. But, more precisely, this incident lit a bonfire that had long been laid: a bonfire built with the tinder of an ever more unbearable — because ever more provocative — occupation, along with the breakdown of the Oslo peace process and the blatant corruption of the leadership of the Palestinian Authority. Sharon tossed a match, and the Al-Aqsa Intifada began. This Intifada was as different from the first Intifada as the first Intifada was from the 1936-1939 uprising. While the first Intifada was a nonviolent grassroots struggle — organized and directed by a "unified leadership," with local committees that together began to structure a civil society — the second Intifada lacked a common vision and direction, and sidelined the majority of the Palestinian people. Most significantly and seriously, this uprising was not an authentic "intifada," inasmuch as it was bent on vengeance.

In response to the outbreak of the second Intifada, on 8 October 2000, the Jerusalem Heads of Churches called for prayers. On 12 October, they led an Ecumenical Prayer Service in St. Stephen's Church on Nablus Road. The statements that followed — a statement on 9 November and a Christmas message, and those issued through 2001 into early 2002 — refer again and again to a "deteriorating" situation. This refrain conveyed a mounting sense of emergency, and reflected the situation on the ground.

The Israeli response to the Al-Aqsa Intifada, particularly after Ariel Sharon came to power in 2001, was intensified brutality. This brutality was, of course, enfolded into responses to the attacks of 11 September and "the worldwide war on terrorism." Under this cover, the Israeli government could and did act with increased impunity to break Palestinian ability to resist. Even more brutal was Israeli action to break the Palestinian *will* to resist, beginning with an unrestrained onslaught on the Palestinian areas in October 2001. At this time, the Jerusalem Heads of Churches issued a particularly urgent call to churches throughout the world and to the entire international community when the Israeli Defense Force (IDF) occupied Bethlehem in October 2001. And lamentation is heard in the 2001 Christmas message of the Jerusalem Heads of Churches: "Time and again, hope has been raised only to be smashed by daily events."

The escalation of violence continued unabated into the new year. Through the months of February and March there was unceasing attack and counterattack. Fatah[3] took up the strategy of Hamas and mounted a suicide-bombing attack; the first one was perpetrated by a female suicide bomber. The IDF carried out operations in the West Bank and Gaza. Suicide bombers from an Al-Aqsa Martyrs' Brigade detonated bombs on a crowded street, in a bus, in a neighborhood, in a restaurant. In March alone, ninety-nine Israelis were killed in seventeen suicide attacks.[4] The last of these attacks was on 27 March in the Park Hotel in Netanya, where several families were gathered to celebrate Passover. Thirty people were killed; 144 were wounded. The attack became known as the "Passover massacre."[5]

Then, on 29 March, the IDF launched Operation Defensive Shield,[6] a series of military raids on Palestinian towns, beginning with Ramallah.[7] Bethlehem was invaded during the night of 2 April 2002.[8] The next morning, on 3 April 2002, the Jerusalem Heads of Churches sent an appeal to President Bush, urging him "to stop immediately the inhuman tragedy that is taking place in this Holy Land in our Palestinian towns and villages. Only this morning the Israeli tanks have reached the Church of the Nativity in Bethlehem, the City of our Lord Jesus Christ." Tanks also tore through side streets of the old city of Bethlehem, leaving a trail of debris and destruction. The Heads of Churches spoke of indiscriminate killing, and of people deprived of water, electricity, food supplies, and medical assistance. They concluded, "We call upon your Christian Conscience — because we know you are the only one who can stop this tragedy immediately." By Easter 2002, the message of the Heads of Churches was a groan: "Father, forgive them, for they know not what they do."[9]

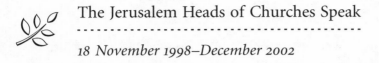

The Jerusalem Heads of Churches Speak

18 November 1998–December 2002

The three Patriarchs of Jerusalem delivered a joint letter to the Israeli Minister of the Interior (and copied to the President of the State and the Prime Minister), requesting that he bring an end to the policy of consistently forfeiting the Jerusalem resident identity cards of Palestinians obliged to settle beyond the municipal limits of the city, primarily because Israeli authorities have refused to grant Palestinians permits to build or expand houses within the Jerusalem region.[10] Cases in which the Jerusalem identity card has been withdrawn have multiplied sixfold within the past two years. The Patriarchs emphasized that this measure has profound repercussions for the entire Palestinian population, but for the Christians in particular, and requested that this policy be brought to an end and that plans be made to return already confiscated cards. [This is a summary; the text is not available.]

18 November 1998

Communique of the Patriarchs of Jerusalem, the Franciscan Custos, and the Heads of Christian Communities in the Holy Land

On 4 April, while some communities were celebrating Easter and others Palm Sunday, very serious incidents took place in Nazareth during which numerous Christians were assaulted and injured. Property was damaged and Christian symbols were desecrated. Worshipers were prevented from attending religious services. An atmosphere of fear has been created.

We, the Patriarchs of Jerusalem, the Franciscan Custos, and the Heads of the Christian Communities in the Holy Land, express our sympathy and solidarity with the entire population of Nazareth and especially with the injured and those who had their property damaged, assuring them of our strong support.

Painful as the situation is, and as a sign of protest and also realizing the inadequate measures taken to guarantee the safety of our people and the pilgrims, we have decided to close the Basilica of the Annunciation and all our Churches in Nazareth on the 6th and 7th of April, except for the liturgical Offices.

This measure might be repeated and even extended should division continue to be provoked among the population of Nazareth by allowing the sentiments of extremists to be aroused and offenses to be committed against Christians.

In spite of what has happened, we repeat our firm will to act with Christian love towards those who have offended us according to justice and mutual respect.

We call on all Christians and Moslems to resort to reason and to help end the violence and to refrain from further acts of hostility, because the end result will neither benefit the Christian nor the Moslem and [the] only loser will be the Holy City of Nazareth.

We urge the Government of Israel to bear its responsibilities and to take the appropriate means to stop the violence and to restore order and security for all and to preserve the sacredness of the City of the Annunciation.

We ask Almighty God to enlighten all and make us instruments of His peace.

5th April 1999

To All Ambassadors, Local Christians, Christian Pilgrims, and Travel Agents in the Holy Land, 4th November 1999

For two thousand years now, the City of Nazareth has been sacred to the Christian world as the site where the biblical event of the Annunciation took place. Ever since the period of Ottoman rule some five hundred years ago, this city has also lived in an atmosphere of peaceful co-existence between Christians and Muslims where the freedoms, rights, and obligations of both parties were studiously observed by all parties. The common bonds that link Christianity and Islam in this city are firm and have made the City of the Annunciation an example of traditional harmony and peace. Those bonds range from religious belief in the Virgin Mary as found in our Holy Books to a fulfillment of our civic responsibilities.

This sense of peaceful co-existence and confident harmony has recently been shaken by a series of sad events that have been painful and counterproductive for the majority of both faith communities. The violent incidents last Easter when the Israeli police force did not initially intervene to control the riots, as well as the insults and injuries directed against many Christians, have unfortunately raised the levels of intolerance and tension further.

Now, and despite the ruling of the court of law in Israel that the land adjacent to the Basilica of the Annunciation is state land, the government has supported a small group of fundamentalists who are intent on building a mosque only a few meters away from the historical Church of the Annunciation in Nazareth.

The Israeli-Ministerial decision to give the go-ahead for the laying of the cornerstone to this construction on 8 November 1999 has been maintained despite numerous and repeated interventions by different ecclesiastical and secular bodies, and perhaps also in spite of the tensions it will inevitably create amongst the one people of Nazareth.

We, the representatives of the Christian Communities in the Holy Land, view this decision with grave concern. Not only is it a clear discrimination against the Christian community in Galilee, it is equally an abandonment of the rule of law by the government and an attempt to promote electoral interests at the expense of the national unity of the Palestinian people across the land.

Consequently, and to express the disapprobation of all the Churches at the way that their rights have been summarily violated, we wish to inform our faithful masses as well as pilgrims that all the Sanctuaries of the Holy Land will be closed on 22 and 23 November 1999. We trust that we do not need to take any further steps in the near future, and that the government will rise to the challenge by applying law and order for all.

We sign this statement today with a heavy heart. We also call upon our Muslim brothers to support us in this action so that what befalls us today will not also befall them tomorrow. We also pray to the Almighty that the wounds of Nazareth will soon be healed, and that it can rediscover its special role as a symbol of the traditional and centuries-long peaceful coexistence between Christians and Muslims, and as [a] stimulus for the peace, which the Holy Land needs so much.

Diodoros I
   Greek Orthodox Patriarch
Michel Sabbah
   Latin Patriarch
Torkom Manoogian
   Armenian Patriarch
Giovanni Battistelli
   Custos of the Holy Land

✐

Message of the Patriarchs and Heads of Christian Communities in Jerusalem on the Occasion of the Great Jubilee in the Year 2000

Beloved Brothers and Sons

1. To you: "Grace, mercy, and peace from God the Father and Christ Jesus our Lord" (2 Timothy 1:2). We addressed our first message to you in 1995 so that we could prepare to welcome the grace of the Great Jubilee of the mystery of the Incarnation and of the Birth of Our Lord and God Jesus Christ. We address this message to you today as we are both celebrating the start of the year of grace and the Jubilee in Bethlehem. We address this message also to the entire world, which looks to our Holy Land and to our Churches, and sees in us the image of the First Church from where the Good News made its way out to the rest of the world.

Mystery of the Incarnation of the Word of God

2. The message for the year 2000 invites us to focus our reflection on the essence of the Jubilee and its primary meaning, that is to say, the anniversary of the mystery of the Incarnation of the Eternal Word of God in our Holy Land. Saint John said: "In the beginning was the Word, and the Word was with God, and the Word was God. . . . And the Word was made flesh, and dwelt among us" (John 1:1, 14). Saint Paul also said: "In the dispensation of the fullness of time," God wanted, in His infinite wisdom and goodness, to "make known unto us the mystery of his will" (Ephesians 1:9). He "spoke unto us by his son, the brightness of his glory and the express image of his person" (Hebrews 1:2-3). Born under the Law, He was "like as we are, yet without sin" (Hebrews 4:15). He freed us from sin, reconciled us with God, and gave us "the power to become the sons of God" (John 1:12). The primary meaning of all the celebrations of the year 2000 is this: We need to prostrate ourselves in adoration before the mystery of God and the mystery of forgiveness and reconciliation that God granted us, rendering us capable of freeing ourselves of the evil in us and around us.

The Great Jubilee

3. Christians in the Holy Land, God has granted us the grace to remain, through the difficulties and vicissitudes of history, His witnesses in the land that is ours. We have persevered and with our prayers, our hopes, and our suffering we have surrounded the places that He sanctified by His birth, His passion, His death, and His glorious Resurrection. Today, He grants us the grace of celebrating together, in the very places of His birth and all His holy places as witnesses of His Salvation, the bimillennial anniversary of His Incarnation, which is simultaneously a privilege and a serious responsibility.

In the Bible, Jubilee has the meaning of the return of man and beast to their Creator. From this come the annulment of various human relationships, and the liberation of man and the earth from any alienation or servitude: "And ye shall hallow the fiftieth year, and proclaim liberty throughout all the land unto all the inhabitants thereof: it shall be a jubilee unto you, and ye shall return every man unto his possession . . ." (Leviticus 25:10). Emancipation means the liberation of man from servitude to and oppression from his brother, as with liberation from servitude to himself, and from sin and from any evil that he harbors within himself.

The verses of Isaiah (61:1-2) read by Jesus in the synagogue of Nazareth, and that He applied to Himself, have the same meaning: "The Spirit of the Lord is upon me, because he hath anointed me to preach the gospel to the poor. He hath sent me to preach deliverance to the captives, and recovering of sight to the blind, to set at liberty those who are oppressed, and to proclaim a year of grace of the Lord." Afterwards, He added: "This day is this scripture fulfilled in your ears" (Luke 4:16-30). Throughout the year 2000, we will meditate on these verses, which will guide us towards true liberty, the liberty that serves the poor, the captives, the blind and oppressed.

How should we celebrate the Jubilee and how should we respond to the grace of God?

4. The Jubilee first invites us to remain in continual conversation with God, to place before Him all our efforts and our labors. We listen to God: "Give ear, O earth, for the Lord hath spoken" (Isaiah 1:2), and God listens to us and answers us: "Thou shalt cry, and he shall say, Here I am" (Isaiah 58:9). We lend our ears to what He says to us in the person through whom His Word has become man. Thus we shall know our faith better, and we shall continue navigating the difficulties of our daily lives.

The Jubilee invites us then to convert: To turn away from our sins and to turn ourselves towards God. The first step to take for this to happen is to recognize that we are sinners, and to have the courage to ask God and each other for forgiveness. The mercy of God is great and passes all understanding. It is He who forgives and who takes pity on all who invoke Him and who return to Him, for "the earth is full of the love of God" (Psalm 32:5). However, in the Lord's Prayer, the forgiveness of God demands that we forgive our brothers and sisters: "Forgive us our debts, as we forgive our debtors" (Matthew 6:12). He who does not forgive his brothers and sisters deprives himself of the forgiveness of God.

On the other hand, God asks us to honestly and frankly confess that we have not perfectly kept "the unity of the Spirit in the bond of peace" throughout our pilgrimage in this Holy Land and that our obedience to the prayer of the Savior at the Last Supper (John 17:9) has been incomplete: "That they all may be one, as thou, Father, art in me, and I in thee, that they also may be one in us, that the world may believe that thou has sent me" (John 17:21). Each of us follows his own path, alone, as if Christ were divided (see 1 Corinthians 1:13). We have become strangers to one another, sometimes even rivals.

God has brought our hearts together in these days: We do not want to remain prisoners of our faults and of our past sins. We do not want to be caught up in events or bitter memories in attempting to justify ourselves or to blame our brothers. Today, we ask God to fill us with his mercy and clemency, to give us the grace to re-read our history together, and to give us in our present lives more love and unity so that we may be "joined together in the same mind and in the same judgment" (1 Corinthians 1:10).

Today, there is among us, by dint of our faith in the very same Jesus Christ, real community, although it may be imperfect. We aspire to become and to one day appear as that which we really are: One body in Christ (see Romans 12:5; 1 Corinthians 12:27), the same house [with] the sentiments of brothers. We will thus begin a new period in our history that will be based upon faith in God and respect for all of God's creatures.

We direct sincere greetings to the Jewish people. All of us today are fighting for justice and peace. Since the seventh century, we have shared a common history, we Jews, Muslims, and Christians. Together, we Jews, Muslims, and Christians have shared the same faith in Abraham, Father of the Prophets. The conflict between Arabs and Jews only began at the start of this century. Today we are called upon to work together to seek out justice and peace for us all. Today, our history is within our hands to shape according to our response to the Christmas message sung by the angels in the heavens above: "Glory to God and peace on earth to all men of goodwill."

A Welcoming Church

5. Finally, we direct our message to the world and to the pilgrims coming to our Churches. The Church of Jerusalem opens its arms to all the Churches. Together, here, we welcome all who come as pilgrims to our land; we surround them with our veneration and we are happy to welcome them. For Jerusalem is the mother of the Churches and "the place where our roots lie, forever living and nourishing. All Christians are born there" (Memorandum, Nov. 1994).

During the Jubilee year, numerous pilgrims will come to the Holy Land to look for the sources of the Spirit and of their faith. There, they hope to find nourishment, not only through their visits and their prayers at the Holy Places, but also and especially by sharing the prayer and testimony of the local Christian communities, because it is by "the living stones that the archaeological holy places come to life" (Ibid.). We welcome them and we share the renewal of their faith and of their path towards forgiveness in our land, which God wanted to be a land of forgiveness and reconciliation with Him and among men. We offer them the constancy of our faith throughout difficulties, and we will profit from the example of their faith. We offer them the example of our love and the unity of our hearts; they will thus discover the mystery of God and His grace in the Holy Places and in the living temples that we are.

Conclusion

6. Our message to our Churches and to the world is a message of faith, hope, and charity. It is a message which welcomes the strengthening of the ties of love between our various Churches and the families of Churches to which we all belong, spread throughout the world. Our message, from Bethlehem, the city of the birth of the Prince of Peace, our Lord and God Jesus Christ, the Eternal Word of God, is a spiritual message directed to the world and to all our faithful in Palestine, Israel, Jordan, and all the Arab countries: May we all live in justice and peace.

The celebration of the Great Jubilee invites us to intensify our efforts in the Holy Land so that our Churches remain faithful to their vocation and to their mission and so that our faithful remain attached to their faith, their liberty, and their aspirations in times that never cease to become more and more difficult. God has summoned us to a difficult life of perpetual combat with ourselves and with all manifestations of evil and oppression in the world. However, God is faithful: If we abide in Him, He will abide in us. Let us not be troubled and let us not be afraid. Jesus said: "Be not afraid. In the world ye shall have tribulation: but be of good cheer; I have overcome the world" (John 16:33).

We ask God, through the intercession of the Virgin Mary in all her purity, that the year to come be a year of grace and goodness, a time of liberty and of new dignity with the blessing of God Almighty, the Father, the Son, and the Holy Spirit, One God. Amen.

+ Diodoros I, Greek Orthodox Patriarch of Jerusalem
+ Michel Sabbah, Latin Patriarch of Jerusalem
+ Torkom Manoogian, Armenian Patriarch of Jerusalem
  Giovanni Battistelli, O.F.M., Custos of the Holy Land
+ [Anba] Abraham, Coptic Orthodox Archbishop
+ Sewerius Mourad, Syrian Orthodox Archbishop
+ Gabriel, Ethiopian Orthodox Archbishop

+ Riah Abu El-Assal, Anglican Bishop
+ Lutfi Laham, Melkite Greek Catholic Patriarchal Vicar
+ Paul Sayah, Maronite Patriarchal Vicar
+ Andre Bedoglouyan, Catholic Armenian Patriarchal Vicar
+ Gregoire Boutros Abdel-Ahad, Syrian Catholic Patriarchal Vicar
+ Mounib Younan, Lutheran Bishop

Bethlehem, 4 December 1999

⁂

Easter Message for the Great Jubilee of the Year 2000

From Their Beatitudes the Patriarchs and
Heads of the Christian Communities in Jerusalem
to
Our Beloved Brothers and Sisters in Christ
in the Holy Land and the World

The last few months have been encouraging to us all in view of the manifestations of solidarity from our Christian family. We inaugurated the celebrations of the third millennium together on 4 December 1999 when the Heads of all the traditional Churches in Jerusalem joined thousands of people from our land and other parts of the world at Manger Square in Bethlehem in a Common Celebration. This special event helped encourage large numbers of pilgrims to travel to the Holy Land in order to witness to Christ and renew their faith in those places from where our Christian faith spread forth to the whole world.

Shortly thereafter, we were richly blessed with the visit of many Heads of Churches. In early January 2000, a great many of the Patriarchs and Archbishops of the Greek Orthodox Church worldwide came to the Holy Land to celebrate Christmas together in Bethlehem. Later that month, in mid-January, the spiritual leader of the Armenian Orthodox Church, His Holiness Karekin II, Catholicos of All Armenians, visited us as well. And it was only a few weeks ago that we welcomed in our midst His Holiness Pope John Paul II and tens of thousands of pilgrims from around the world who accompanied him on his spiritual pilgrimage to our land.

All these events have given witness to the life and presence of the local Christian Church in our land and strengthened hope for our future despite the arduous journey along the pathway to peace.

The reason for the Millennium is the anniversary of the birth of the Holy Child of Bethlehem. Now, as we approach the commemoration of the Passion, Death, and Resurrection of our Lord and Savior Jesus Christ, we have the opportunity to focus attention on the basic tenets of our Christian faith.

We remember today St. Paul affirming to us, "All I want is to know Christ and to experience the power of his Resurrection, to share in his sufferings and become like him in his death, in the hope that I myself will be raised from death to life" (Phil. 3:10-11). The world might disappoint human beings. It might disillusion them when it attempts to denigrate the eternal values that Jesus exemplified to us throughout his ministry. But we are called to be witnesses of the Risen Christ. We need to demonstrate our commitment to Christ in clear and meaningful words.

Like Pontius Pilate in front of Jesus, many people ask today, "And what is truth?" (Jn. 18:38). As witnesses to our faith, we have to spell out our conviction that God's truth is vital to our daily life. Jesus said, "I am the way, the truth, and the life" (Jn. 14:6). By following the truth, we must emphasize the importance of sincerity and the need for compassion amongst human beings. As such, we ask all of you, clergy and laity alike, individuals or organizations, to love one another, to understand each other, and to work together in order to preserve Jesus' teachings and to uphold those principles for which he gave his life. Then we will indeed prove that his death on the Cross was not in vain, nor was the power of his glorious Resurrection diluted over the centuries.

All these events took place in the Holy City of Jerusalem, which is at the heart of our Holy Land. We hope that all religious and secular authorities will work unstintingly to remove those obstacles that come in the way of a comprehensive and just peace for our region. And no matter how difficult the times ahead, we encourage you to remain steeped in your faith so that you can "have the righteousness that is given through faith in Christ" (Phil. 3:9) and that you can truly proclaim Jesus' statement to his disciples, "Be brave, I have defeated the world!" (Jn. 16:33). Then you can truly cry out loud in jubilation, Christ is Risen! He is Risen Indeed! Hallelujah!

The Jerusalem Heads of Churches Speak

Their Beatitudes the Patriarchs and Heads of the Christian Communities in Jerusalem

+ Diodoros I, Greek Orthodox Patriarch
+ Michel Sabbah, Latin Patriarch
+ Torkom II, Armenian Orthodox Patriarch
   Fr. Giovanni Battistelli, Custos of the Holy Land
+ Anba Abraham, Coptic Orthodox Archbishop
+ Swerios Malki Mourad, Syrian Orthodox Patriarchal Vicar
+ Gabriel, Ethiopian Orthodox Archbishop
+ Riah Abu El-Assal, Anglican Bishop
+ Mounib Younan, Lutheran Bishop
+ Boulos Sayyah, Maronite Patriarchal Vicar
+ Gregorios Boutros Abdul Ahhad, Syrian Catholic Patriarchal Vicar
+ Andre Bedoghlian, Armenian Catholic Patriarchal Vicar

&

Statement Release (fragment)

In the name of the thirteen Heads of the Churches of the Holy Land, we want to assure you[11] that our sincere prayer and ardent hope will accompany you on your trip to the United States. The path to peace will not be easy, and the process of arriving at this peace is not much easier. However, we wish that the expectations of millions of Israelis and Palestinians will be met this week with a meeting of the minds and the hearts that will prepare the path to a truly peaceful and just future for the two peoples and the three religions of the land blessed by the Prophets. We beseech you to put all the effort that you possibly can into your deliberations in order to seek a path to peace.

15 July 2000

Greek Orthodox Patriarch of Jerusalem
Latin Patriarch of Jerusalem
Armenian Patriarch of Jerusalem

Letter to the Camp David Leaders

HE Mr. Bill Jefferson Clinton
President of the United States

HE Mr. Ehud Barak
Prime Minister of Israel

HE Mr. Yasser Arafat
President of the PNA

Greetings to you from Jerusalem as you strive to bring peace to our beloved Holy Land. We continue to pray that you will succeed in your prophetic mission of ending the long and painful conflict in our region. Yours
is a difficult and challenging task, and we remain confident that you will
conclude it in a manner that lifts up the hopes of the two peoples and three
religions of this land — Palestinians and Israelis, Jews, Christians, and
Muslims alike.

Your Excellencies, it is an established fact that our Patriarchates and
Churches enjoy a long history and a rich heritage in this biblical land. Local Christians have been represented by the ecclesiastical institutions here
for centuries, and have enjoyed special privileges that were codified by the
"Status Quo" provisions as much as by custom and tradition over many
centuries. As you deliberate over those issues that impact the Holy City of
Jerusalem, we trust you will not forget or overlook our age-long presence
here. The rich tapestry of this land is made even richer and more precious
with this continuous Christian life, witness, and presence alongside the
two other Abrahamic traditions of Judaism and Islam.

Conscious of this qualitative and quantitative reality as represented by
all our Christian communities, we appeal to you as foremost political leaders and negotiators to ensure that the Christian communities within the
walls of the Old City are not separated from each other. We regard the
Christian and Armenian Quarters of the Old City as inseparable and continuous entities that are firmly united by the same faith. Furthermore, we
trust that your negotiators will also secure that any arrangement for Jerusalem will ensure that the fundamental freedoms of worship and access by

all Christians to their Holy Sanctuaries and to their headquarters within the Old City are not impeded in any way whatsoever. Such freedoms underline the special nature of this city and enhance its right development.

We suggest that one possible way of enduring peaceful unity and cohesive prosperity of the Christian presence in the Holy City of Jerusalem — with its varied mosaic of worshipers, churches, and sanctuaries — is through a system of international guarantees that will ensure to the three religious communities a quality of right of access to their respective Holy Places, of profession of faith, and of development.

Your Excellencies, as Heads of our Churches and being fully conscious of the heavy duty we carry with us, we also suggest that it might well be advisable to have representatives from our three Patriarchates and the Custody of the Holy Land at the Camp David summit meeting as much as at any future fora in order to provide continuity and consultation on our future and on our rights so that our one collective presence here — with [its] history of rights and expectations — is maintained unequivocally and safeguarded fully.

In conclusion, and as we reiterate our prayers for the success of your summit meeting, we also recall that Jerusalem — Al-Quds the Sacred and Yerushalaim the Peaceful — will remain vital to Jews, Christians, and Muslims alike. And, in so being, it will reflect a sense of full equality for all the three religions witnessing in this land.

    (Signed by)
+ Diodoros I
    Greek Orthodox Patriarch
+ Michel Sabbah
    Latin Patriarch
+ Torkom II
    Armenian Orthodox Patriarch

17 July 2000

Heads of Christians in Jerusalem

Statement of Their Beatitudes the Patriarchs and Heads of Christian Communities in Jerusalem

30 September 2000

With a resolute Christian faith that is predicated upon the teachings of our Lord Jesus Christ, and which calls for love, forgiveness, and fellowship, we express our deep sorrow at the painful events that occurred at the Haram al-Sharif on midday, 29 September 2000. We offer our sincerest condolences to the whole Palestinian people in general and to the bereaved families in particular, and denounce the aggression of the sanctuary of a holy place in Jerusalem. We consider that such a violation is tantamount to a violation on any and all Christian and Muslim holy sites, and affirm our solidarity with the Palestinian people, Muslims and Christians alike, in defending their fundamental rights of worship and prayer in Jerusalem.[12] In so doing, we also reject any provocation against the feelings of the faithful irrespective of its nature, shape, or presence.

We re-affirm hereby our Christian position, as we have done time and again in our previous statements, of the need to ensure the freedom of movement, access, worship, and prayer, as much as the need to put an end to the violations against all holy places in Jerusalem. We call for the implementation of all relevant and binding resolutions that reflect the principles of international legitimacy, and particularly those related to Jerusalem,[13] in order to secure a comprehensive, just, and lasting peace for the peoples of all the three monotheistic religions in the Holy Land.

"How wonderful it is, how pleasant, for God's people to live together in harmony!" Ps. 133:1[14]

Peace, Born of Justice —
The Churches Call for Peace in the Holy Land

On 9 November 2000, the three Patriarchs (Greek Orthodox, Armenian, and Latin), the Custos of the Holy Land, and representatives of nine other Christian Churches of Jerusalem signed a call for peace in the Holy Land. Here is the text of that message:

> "They think to soothe the hurts of my people by flippantly saying: 'Peace, Peace!', whereas there is really no peace."

On 28 September 2000, the provocative visit of the leader of Likud, the Israeli opposition party, to the esplanade of the Al-Haram al-Sharif in Jerusalem provoked a new Palestinian uprising in the Holy Land. This incident, like the events that followed, should have been a clear warning to . . . the Israelis as well as the Palestinian leadership of the pressing necessity of continued vigilance over the peace process and of the need to resolve all pending problems — including the matter of Jerusalem. However, Israel has preferred to respond with recourse to an even greater use of force.

Fully cognizant of our duty as religious leaders, we look with infinite pain and sadness upon the deaths, the injuries, and the maiming caused by this most recent uprising. Although both peoples have been affected by the events of the last five weeks, we cannot help but note how much the overwhelming majority of the victims has been on the Palestinian side. We extend to all of them our profound solidarity and sympathy, and we offer our condolences to the families of all who — young or old — have lost their lives or have been injured. We sincerely think that it is high time to put an end to this spiraling drama of reciprocated violence.

We emphasize that the rights of one people are also the rights of any other. The Palestinians should have the opportunity to enjoy total security and to protect their interests and those of their people, just as Israel should be able to enjoy total security and to protect its interests and those of its people. Both peoples could then live side by side in peace, each in their own sovereign state, without being a source of fear for the other. But inasmuch as people continue to be the victims of injustice, they will continue to be a source of fear and insecurity for their neighbors.

Implementing the Resolutions

The Church thinks that it is the right and the duty of an occupied people to fight against injustice in order to obtain peace, believing at the same time that nonviolent methods of resistance remain stronger and more effective. And so, the two parties must show the necessary courage, in heart as well as in mind, to study the root of the conflict, such that the Palestinian people can finally obtain full freedom within their own tangible State. Now and most urgently, it is absolutely necessary to put into place principles of international legitimacy in implementing the resolutions and commitments of the U.N. Security Council. Such courage is proof of wisdom and clairvoyance, and is a preliminary condition indispensable to the establishment of a lasting peace.

We remain convinced that one day justice will finally prevail and that the violence will ineluctably cease. Only then will the two peoples be able to reunite in reconciliation. Moreover, it would be more reasonable and courageous to head straight towards dialogue that would guarantee peace that relied upon components of justice, security, and dignity so that we would no longer have to live through such violence and such painful events.

Today, from the Holy City of Jerusalem, we express our ardent desire to see peace, justice, equality, and security established between Palestinians and Israelis, in this Holy Land wherein God chose to reveal His Wisdom to human beings. We call upon all Orthodox, Catholic, and Protestant Churches everywhere in the world, and on all *"the friends of peace"* in our country, in this region, and in the world over to work together in order to establish complete, just, and lasting peace between Israelis and Palestinians. Peace and justice are the absolute and inviolate right of the two peoples of this land. Peace must not be sacrificed on the altar of political pride. For in the final analysis, peace can only be born of justice.

"Some trust in chariots, and some in horses: but we will remember the name of the LORD our God" (Ps. 20:7).

Common Christmas Message 2000 of Their Beatitudes the Patriarchs and Heads of the Christian Communities in the Holy Land

17 December 2000

> "By the tender mercy of our God, the dawn from on high will break upon us, to give light to those who sit in darkness, and in the shadow of death, to guide our feet into the way of peace." Lk. 1:78-79

Greetings in the Name of Our Lord Jesus Christ to All Our Beloved Brothers and Sisters!

In the year 2000, our land — the land of Jesus' birth — cries out in pain again. The year started with an outpouring of joy as we all came together to celebrate the new millennium. We then moved onward with our faith and prayers, raising our own expectations as much as those of our people, that peace with justice for Palestinians and Israelis was at long last within grasp. But in the last few months,[15] hope has been replaced with fear, despair, pain, loss, and death. Stones and shells are competing unequally on a daily basis. Palestinians and Israelis are living once again with the painful realities of violence, terror, injustice, closures, insecurity, and dehumanization. For many of us, a reality of peace-filled co-existence has become more challenging and distant. In such circumstances, hope has also become a forlorn and ever-arduous task. Yet, with our faith and confidence in the One whose birth we celebrate, we re-commit ourselves to hope and re-dedicate ourselves to continue working for justice and peace.

As pastors of our Christian people, we are deeply aware of those sad realities. We bear in our hearts and minds the pain of our own communities as well as that of all Palestinian and Israeli men and women of faith in our land. We remain conscious that our people will not enjoy many of the customary Christmas celebrations in this land this year. Yet, we urge them not to lose sight of that event in Bethlehem some two thousand years ago. We urge the leaders of the international community to help all those fighting to tackle the root causes of the conflict, and to give back to the Palestinian people their freedom and dignity so that the Israeli people can then enjoy security and tranquility. This is the message of the Christians of the Holy Land to the Christian world today.

The basis of our hope lies in God's faithfulness and truth. We trust in his steadfast mercy. Christmas points us beyond the painful realities of the moment toward the power, the light, and the love of God which guides every human being to truth, justice, and dignity. This love, made manifest at Christmas, cannot keep us complacent. Rather, it is meant to sustain us as we seek to live in ways which bring healing, wholeness, and justice to all peoples of the world. Despite the brokenness and pain which exist in our world today, the gift of Christmas reminds us that God remains greater than all human power and all human principalities in our region as much as in the whole world.

For us all, the birth of our Lord and Savior represents the one light that dispels darkness. We are called to live as children of the light, marching ever onward on the way of justice and peace, for that is where we are supposed to discover life, joy, and fulfillment, even if we never achieve peace in our own lifetime.

Today, we need to find ways in our own hearts and minds where we can nurture a culture of peace. We have heard and accepted the gospel of the peace of Christ, and we are his witnesses and ambassadors who are entrusted with the message of reconciliation (2 Cor. 5:18-20). Indeed, as we celebrate the birth of the Prince of Peace (Isa. 9:6), the one who reconciled us to God and gave each one of us the power to reconcile with his brother and sister, we pray that hostility, bitterness, and alienation may be swept away.

As we prepare ourselves to receive the new-born in a lowly manger at Bethlehem, we invite all our sons and daughters to join us in our religious celebrations as we pray for those who are dead, bereaved, afflicted, and injured so that God will bless us all with an even deeper faith and comfort us with his healing power. We invite them also to be patient and to rekindle their hope in the face of all difficulties, so that this very hope may become an in-breaking of light and a resurgence of faith. In so doing, we, not unlike the shepherds, can go forth into the darkest of nights, glorifying and praising God, who came to save humankind and to fill the earth with justice and peace.

Holy Christmas and a Blessed New Year.

Statement by Heads of Christian Churches in Jerusalem

As we are concerned for the spiritual well-being, the mental health, and the security of all citizens of this Holy Land — Christian, Muslim, and Jew alike — we are calling upon the Israeli Government, the Palestinian Authority, and upon religious and secular world leaders, as well as upon all men and women of goodwill, to bring a rapid end to the conflict that threatens the lives of thousands of inhabitants in this Land.

We are convinced that peace negotiations between Israelis and Palestinians are the only way to ensure the well-being of our peoples.

We believe that the violence, which has intensified over these last months, will only end when each of the two conflicting parties makes a genuine effort to respect the respective rights of the other, thereby affirming the dignity and the value of each and every human life (be it that of a man, a woman, or a child). We respectfully request that all of our people be protected, in such a way so as to re-establish mutual trust and security for Israelis and Palestinians.

24 March 2001

Common Easter Message by Their Beatitudes the Patriarchs and Their Excellencies the Heads of the Churches of Jerusalem

"Christ is risen" (Luke 24:1-52). Jesus, Lord and Savior, has risen today, just as he had foretold his apostles. "They will put him to death, and on the third day he will rise again" (Mt. 17:23). Indeed, after the suffering and death of our Lord Jesus Christ, the Churches of Jerusalem witness with one voice and one heart to the glory of his Resurrection as they rejoice in the hope and strength that come from that empty tomb in the heart of our Holy City.

Before bearing the cross himself, Jesus had called upon his disciples to carry the cross and follow him. He had asked them to walk the narrow path that leads toward salvation. This double vision of the cross and the resurrection applies to the situation in which we find ourselves today. Our suffering and fear in the past few months have increased in view of the uncertainty of the political situation. We reassure each and every one of our sons and daughters that we share the pain of every family that is deprived of hope as they go through their daily lives without jobs and income or are exposed physically and psychologically to the painful measures that are imposed upon them. Although the closures that are sealing most of the Palestinian territories bring days of deep despair, we ought to remain committed to hope. "I call heaven and earth to witness against you today, that I have set before you life and death, blessing and curses. Choose life, so that you and your descendants may live" (Deut. 30:19).

In this cycle of struggle and suffering, we detect also the way of the cross that will ultimately lead toward the glory of the Resurrection. Thus, celebrating Easter means the restoration of our hope that victory of life over death also will be witnessed in the troubled land of ours. This will only happen when violence and discrimination give way for a real peace between the "two peoples and the three religions" of this small land where God chose to reveal his divine will. Such a peace can only be secured through mutual reconciliation based on the respect for the dignity and value God has given to all human beings. In no way can this peace be imposed by sheer force: it is nurtured by an honest application of justice and mercy in line with internationally accepted legitimate resolutions for the benefit of the weaker part. Therefore, all of us, who claim faith in the Living God who has overcome death and sin, are called today to witness and work with steadfast determination and persistent commitment. The words of the prophet Isaiah come fittingly to mind: "See, the former things have come to pass, and new things I now declare: before they spring forth I tell you of them . . ." (Isaiah 42:9). God speaks to us of a time in which the relationship of creation with the Creator is restored, justice is the benchmark of every nation, and the light of redemption shines in the deepest corners of despair.

As all the Churches of Jerusalem celebrate the paschal festivities together this first year of the new millennium, they also affirm that the experience of Easter is one of liberation. It is a triumph of life over death, of peace over violence. Looking at the One God who manifested his power over servitude and death, we address all secular and political authorities to welcome into their hearts the goodwill and good faith that builds new generations with renewed hope and sustained confidence.

Today, we ask our faithful in the Holy Land as well as all believers worldwide to share with us in the transformation of hearts and minds so that the true joy that comes with the Risen Lord can also infuse their own lives. We pray for an end to the unjustifiable deaths that plague our societies. We pray for the immediate end of all collective punishments, especially for the lifting of the closures of Palestinians' towns and villages. We pray for the goodwill of Palestinians and Israelis — of Jews, Christians. and Moslems alike — in actively working for justice and peace. We pray for equality so that one no longer sees the neighbor as an enemy but rather as a brother or sister with whom to build a new society. Ours is a message of hope and compassion, of reconciliation and joy. To all, we affirm that Easter is the time to become one voice and one heart before the Lord so that "we may come to know him and the power of the Resurrection" (Phil. 3:10) in a genuine, just, and comprehensive peace that no longer disparages one God-given life over another.

Our Christian message remains constant year in, year out. Life conquers death, and love defeats hatred. Hope tramples desolation, joy overcomes despair, and peace ends violence. So let us all proclaim together: "Where, O death, is your victory? Where, O death, is your sting? . . . But thanks [be] to God, who gives us the victory through our Lord Jesus Christ" (1 Cor. 15:55-57).

The Lord is risen! He is risen indeed.

Patriarchs and Heads of the Churches of Jerusalem

15 April 2001

A Call to Prayer by the Heads of the Churches in Jerusalem

7 August 2001

> Jesus said: "Peace I leave with you; my peace I give you. Do not let your heart be troubled, or afraid." (John 14:27)

We are greatly concerned at the deteriorating situation in the Occupied Territories of the Holy Land. Many families have been made homeless; the closures have turned towns and cities into detention camps; the number of unemployed has risen dramatically, resulting in tens of thousands hungry for their daily bread; whilst our children are confronted daily with a picture of bloodshed, violence, assassinations, and murder.

Hatred and a desire for revenge are rampant on both sides — Israeli and Palestinian.

We call upon all our people, throughout this Land, to join us in intensifying our prayers for peace, with justice, and reconciliation. To this end we have arranged a period of daily PRAYER FOR PEACE at 6 p.m. from Wednesday, August 15th, to Tuesday, August 28th, in the churches across the city.

We appeal also to our brothers and sisters around the world — many of whom have already offered generous support — to link their prayers with ours at this special time.

+ *The Patriarchs and Heads of Churches, Communities, and Institutions in Jerusalem*

Prayers for Peace
Jerusalem, 15 August to 28 August
Daily at 6 p.m.

A Message to Churches Worldwide and to the International Community

We, the Patriarchs and the Heads of Churches in Jerusalem, appeal to our Brothers and Sisters around the world to help in a time of urgent need in the Holy Land.

Following the targeted killings, there has been a dramatic intervention, within the last few hours, in the Autonomous Palestinian Territories by the Israeli Armed Forces. Tanks are everywhere; buildings have been sieged; some areas are under curfew; and there is extensive shooting.

We are particularly concerned about Bethlehem (the place of our Savior's birth), with Beit Jala and Beit Sahour, Aida Refugee Camp, Al-Bireh, Ramallah, Jenin, Nablus, and Gaza. The restrictions on movement preventing people [from] going to work, attending school, and even university mean that charitable institutions, hospitals, etc. . . . are placed under great strain to care for residents and patients. Children everywhere are being traumatized.

At a time when Western leaders are concerned with fighting terrorism, it seems that Palestinian residents (both Moslem and Christian) are subjected to similar acts [of] which the world takes little notice.

Whilst we deplore all acts of violence, we appeal to World Church Leaders and the International Community to make urgent representation to the Israeli Government to bring this intolerable situation[16] to an immediate end and begin the process of negotiations in order to work towards a peaceful and a just solution.

+ Patriarch Irenios I: Greek Orthodox Patriarchate
+ Patriarch Michel Sabbah: Latin Patriarchate
+ Patriarch Torkom II: Armenian Apostolic Orthodox Patriarchate
   Father Giovanni Battistelli: Custody of the Holy Land
+ Anba Abraham: Coptic Orthodox Patriarchate
+ Swerios Malki Mourad: Syrian Orthodox Patriarchate
+ Abba Cuostos: Ethiopian Orthodox Patriarchate
+ Riah Abu Al-Assal: Episcopal Church of Jerusalem and the Middle East
+ Mounib Younan: Evangelical Lutheran Church
+ Archimandrite Nabil Safieh: Greek Catholic (Melkite) Patriarchal Exarchate

Jerusalem, October 19, 2001

Statement of the Leaders of the Christian Churches in Jerusalem on the Projected Mosque in Nazareth

We, the leaders of the Christian Churches in the Holy Land, are alarmed by recent developments on the ground, and are once more now urgently demanding that the Government of Israel revoke without further delay its decision to build a mosque on State land right in front of the Shrine of the

Annunciation in Nazareth. This Government project contradicts the original plan made by the Arab Mayor of Nazareth, Tawfiq Zayad, to beautify the city in preparation for the year 2000. That plan designated the same State-owned land for a public square, a pleasant place of meeting for the city's Christian and Muslim inhabitants, and for the gathering of the pilgrims, facilitating their access to the Shrine. It is this plan that we are demanding the Government to respect and to implement.

We are surprised and distressed to see that promises and assurances given us by Government representatives have not been honored, and that the requests, appeals, and protests of the Christian Churches in the Holy Land and throughout the world have been treated with virtual contempt.

The mosque the Government approves to be built is not welcome to the Muslim religious and national authorities themselves, either in the Holy Land or elsewhere in the world. The Government approves and encourages the building of an unneeded mosque right in front of one of the holiest Shrines of Christendom — to which access is already all too difficult and uncertain. [This] is an ill-advised plan of certain Israeli political circles, who are making use of a marginal group of Muslims in order to sow division between Christians and Muslims in Israel, and among Muslims themselves. We specifically recall that leading authorities in the Muslim world have warned against this, even as they have expressed their criticism of this project, and of its divisive intent and effect, and their solidarity with us.

We know for certain that a great majority of our Jewish friends, in Israel and elsewhere, are also firmly opposed to this incomprehensible Government decision.

It is evident that we wholeheartedly support every just expectation of Muslims in Israel to see their right to religious freedom fully respected. We know that there are dozens of ruined, or semi-ruined, mosques and Muslim cemeteries in Israel that Muslim movements and associations seek to restore, and we suggest that the Government, before initiating an unnecessary new mosque right in front of the Shrine of the Annunciation, permit first of all Israeli Muslims to restore their damaged religious heritage, and to take control directly of the Muslim religious property now in Government hands.

We know that our Jewish friends would be deeply concerned about the destructive effects that the Government decision for Nazareth could have on the fruits of decades of hard work to build up and expand Jewish-

93

Christian dialogue. We are therefore particularly confident in appealing for support of Jewish religious leaders and Jewish organizations, in Israel and worldwide.

We feel obliged to observe that, if some Israeli authorities abuse their governmental powers to manipulate people's religious sentiments, to divide the population, to create conflict, to foment intolerant fundamentalism, then they cannot credibly claim that they can be trusted to respect any religion's Holy Places in their jurisdiction, whether in Nazareth or elsewhere. Indeed, we recall that U.N. General Assembly Resolution 181 (II) of 29 November 1947[17] foresaw international guarantees for all Holy Places throughout the Holy Land. As the present case proves, such guarantees may now be more necessary than ever.

Finally, we renew our appeal with a greater sense of urgency than ever to the Government of Israel to revoke a decision that may have incalculable consequences on many levels, and we are asking all Christians and Muslims throughout the world to join us in this effort, and to do so now.

Patriarch Irenios I: Greek Orthodox Patriarchate
Patriarch Michel Sabbah: Latin Patriarchate
Patriarch Torkom II: Armenian Apostolic Orthodox Patriarchate
Father Giovanni Battistelli: Custody of the Holy Land
Anba Abraham: Coptic Orthodox Patriarchate
Bishop Swerios Malki Mourad: Syrian Orthodox Patriarchate
Abba Cuostos: Ethiopian Orthodox Patriarchate
Bishop Paul Nabil Sayyah: Maronite Patriarchal Exarchate
Bishop Riah Abu Al-Assal: Episcopal Church of Jerusalem and the
    Middle East
Bishop Mounib Younan: Lutheran Evangelical Church
Archimandrite Mtanios Haddad: Greek Catholic Patriarchal
    Exarchate
Bishop Andre Dikran Bedoghlyan: Armenian Catholic Patriarchal
    Exarchate
Fr. Elias Tabban: Syrian Catholic Patriarchate

28 November 2001

Christmas Message 2001 by Their Beatitudes the Patriarchs and All the Heads of the Christian Churches in Jerusalem

"So then, brethren, stand firm and hold to the traditions you were taught . . . and may Our Lord Jesus Christ himself, and God our Father, who loved us and gave us eternal comfort and good hope through grace, comfort your hearts." (2 Thess. 2:15-17)

Dear Sisters and Brothers in Jesus Christ,

In the name of Our Lord Jesus Christ we greet all of you in this Holy Land. We wish you all a Blessed Christmas and hope that this solemnity will bring us justice and peace. We pray and ask God to grant this precious gift to our troubled Land, to our suffering people and to all the inhabitants in their determined effort towards a just and lasting peace.

We approach the Divine Infant's manger deeply conscious of the sufferings many of you have been called to endure in these past months and are still enduring, whether through bereavement, injury, unemployment, or a multitude of cares and anxieties. Time and again, hope has been raised only to be smashed by daily events. All around us, we still see violence and injustice. We observe total disregard for the dignity and worth of humankind as well as injustices and humiliation. All of this we deplore. All of which we believe is contrary to the will of God and the teaching of Our Lord Jesus Christ.

In recent weeks we have attempted to play our modest part in trying to encourage the resumption of serious peace negotiations; to draw the world's attention to the suffering and hardships faced by so many in this Land and to safeguard the dignity of the Holy Places, now and especially in the future status of Jerusalem, as well as the rights of the Christian communities and churches around them.

Today, we renew our appeal to the political leaders in this Holy Land to stop all kinds of violence. So let us start a new era of justice and peace that sees both the Palestinian and Israeli peoples, within recognized borders, enjoying safety and tranquility. We launch also an urgent appeal to the International Community to have enough courage to make the right decisions and implement them and so help our peoples to work on their fulfillment.

*   *   *

Dear Sisters and Brothers,

We have called you and all World Churches to pray for the establishment of justice and peace. You responded to our call and so we prayed together and we asked God to have mercy on his Holy City and all its inhabitants. A few weeks ago, we asked you to join us in our "Solidarity Convoy for Peace" to Bethlehem on the occasion of the hard times that Bethlehem and Christ's manger had to pass through. Again you answered our invitation, and we walked to demonstrate our will of peace built on justice and truth according to the angels' song over Bethlehem.

Now, as the Holy Season of Christmas approaches, we would encourage every one of you to stand firm in faith and rooted in your land with the fullness of Christmas joy in your heart, as we tell you with Saint Paul: "Stand firm and hold to the traditions you were taught" (2 Thess. 2:15). We believe God gave us so much when He gave us Jesus, born in Bethlehem's stable. As the Holy Child grew into manhood and on through his Ministry, he revealed to us so much that was in the Father's heart: "No one has ever seen God; it is the only Son who is close to the Father's heart who has made him known" (Jn. 1:18), and he taught us how to see God's will through what happens around us.

Therefore, through our history full of death, destruction, and injustice, we can still see God's love for us and for his human children. His love strengthens us and renews our hope, so we persevere in our search for peace and justice. For this reason, despite all the sufferings and sorrows around us, we must celebrate with joy this Christmas. We must pray too that there will be found, on earth, men and women of goodwill who will listen to the message of the Angels at our Savior's Birth: "Glory to God in the highest, and on earth peace among men with whom he is well pleased" (Lk. 2:14), and work for God's peace especially in this Holy Land. We must also take great care to direct our children, many of whom have been traumatized by the experience of the past days, towards God's love and care for them, so helping them towards a personal relationship to our Father in heaven and to love all their neighbors through the Infant Jesus in his manger, who was born to save all of humanity.

From Bethlehem, the city of the Nativity of Our Lord, we greet our Churches and all our friends across the world and ask that in the midst of their prayers and celebrations, they might remember their brothers and sisters with their many needs here in this Holy Land. We also call all our children to accompany their prayers with charity and awareness of the other's needs. We shall pray as well for the dear pilgrims and tell them that the Holy Land is in urgent need to see strong and courageous pilgrims come and witness through their presence, their faith, and [their] prayer to its sanctity and message of peace.

*   *   *

Dear Sisters and Brothers,

We all shall gather around the manger in Bethlehem but also in our cities and in all other localities and shall sing again the songs of love and hope whilst renewing our belief that our Land will some day enjoy justice and peace. May the eyes and hearts of many open to see that injustice should make place for justice and freedom for all. For this we shall pray as we pray for our Authorities and for the two peoples to understand that they can live together in peace and that they are called to build together the new society that God wants for the land He has blessed. May Almighty God hear and answer our prayer so that this Land and its entire people may know his love, joy, justice, and peace!

May the Lord grant you all a Blessed Christmas and every hope for the New Year, and may God the Father, the Son and the Holy Spirit bless you!

+ Ireneus, Greek Orthodox Patriarch of Jerusalem
+ Michel Sabbah, Latin Patriarch of Jerusalem
+ Torkom Manoogian, Armenian Orthodox Patriarch of Jerusalem
   Fr. Giovanni Battistelli, O.F.M., Custos of the Holy Land
+ Anba Abraham, Coptic Archbishop of Jerusalem
+ Swerios Malki Murad, Syrian Orthodox Archbishop of Jerusalem
+ Abba Cuostos, Ethiopian Archbishop of Jerusalem
+ Paul Sayyah, Maronite Archbishop in the Holy Land
+ Riah Abu El-Assal, Anglican Bishop in Jerusalem
+ Munib Younan, Bishop of the Lutheran Church in Jerusalem
   Archim. Mtanios Haddad, Greek Melkite Catholic Patr. Vicar in
      Jerusalem
   Msgr. George Makhzoum, Armenian Catholic Patr. Vicar in
      Jerusalem
   Fr. Elias Tabban, for the Syrian Catholic Patr. Vicariate in Jerusalem

⊕

A CALL FROM THE HEADS OF CHURCHES IN JERUSALEM TO ALL THE PEOPLE IN THIS HOLY LAND, PALESTINIANS AND ISRAELIS

Jerusalem, March 9, 2002

> "There is a time for killing, a time for healing; a time for knocking down, a time for building; . . . a time for throwing stones away, a time for gathering them; . . . a time for war, a time for peace." (Eccl. 3:3-8)

We, the Patriarchs and the Heads of Churches in this Land, are concerned for the recent developments and the spiral[ing] violence directly affecting the lives of the people. We are distressed to find that the bloodshed is increasing in this country. We are saddened to see more widows, orphans, mourning fathers and mothers on both sides. We deplore the increase of injured people because of killing, shelling, bombarding, violence, and incursion. We ask, "Is this the future that we all want for our children?"

We believe that the key to a just peace is in the hands of both the Israeli Government and the Palestinian Authority. War, shelling, and destruction will not bring justice and security; rather, [they] will intensify hatred and bitterness. We believe that Israeli and Palestinian peoples are called to be partners in an historic peace.

We would confirm that we care for the security of both peoples, just as we care for the security of every human being. But the way the present Israeli Government is dealing with the situation makes neither for security nor for a just peace. We believe that the Israeli security is dependent on the Palestinian freedom and justice. For this reason, we join our voices with every Israeli and Palestinian seeking for a just peace. We ask everyone to take the appropriate measures to stop further massacres or tragedies for our two peoples. We want to say a frank, honest word to the Israeli conscience and the Israeli Government, asking that you stop all kinds of destruction and death caused by the heavy Israeli weaponry. What assurance can be offered to a people deprived of freedom, self-determination, sovereignty, and equality with every Israeli citizen?

To the Palestinian people we urge an end of every kind of violent response. We believe that the way of peace is the way of negotiation. If there is a strong will for making peace, all the pending disputed problems will find a dignified solution.

We appeal to the Israeli people to work for their security in such a way that is just and in which the Palestinians may enjoy their rights as represented in the International Legitimacy. We ask you in the name of the Living God, whom we all worship, to raise your voice for justice, peace, and reconciliation, which are the cry of the soul of all peoples of the world. Inspired by the words of King Solomon in Ecclesiastes, we can say: "We have tried war, stones, killing, and destruction all the period of the conflict. The time has come for peace, justice, and the collecting of stones for building, reconciliation, and healing." Our prayers for peace are more urgently needed than ever.

Know that we have contacted our partner churches abroad with their respective governments to seek their assistance in our quest for peace.

"I will hear what God proclaims; for he proclaims peace to his people, and to his faithful ones, and to those who put in him their hope." (Ps. 85:8)

+ Patriarch Irenios I: Greek Orthodox Patriarch
+ Patriarch Michel Sabbah: Latin Patriarch
+ Patriarch Torkom II: Armenian Apostolic Orthodox Patriarch
  Father Giovanni Battistelli, O.F.M.: Custos of the Holy Land
+ Anba Abraham: Coptic Orthodox Archbishop
+ Swerios Malki Mourad: Syrian Orthodox Archbishop
+ Abba Cuostos: Ethiopian Orthodox Archbishop
+ Paul Nabil Sayyah: Maronite Patriarchal Exarch
+ Bishop Riah Abu Al-Assal: Episcopal Church Bishop of Jerusalem
+ Bishop Mounib Younan: Lutheran Evangelical Bishop
+ Archimandrite Mtanious Haddad: Greek Catholic Patriarchal
    Exarch
+ Georges Khazzoum: Armenian Catholic Patriarchal Exarch
  Fr. Elias Tabban: for the Syrian Catholic Exarchate

Urgent Appeal from the Patriarchs and Heads of Churches in Jerusalem

To President George Bush

Tuesday, April 03, 2002

Mr. President,

We appeal to you to stop immediately the inhuman tragedy that is taking place in this Holy Land in our Palestinian towns and villages. Only this morning the Israeli tanks have reached the Church of the Nativity in Bethlehem, the City of our Lord Jesus Christ.

There is wanton indiscriminate killing. Very many people are deprived of water, electricity, food supplies, and basic medical needs. Many of our religious institutions have been invaded and damaged. We call upon your Christian Conscience — because we know you are the only one who can stop this tragedy immediately.[18]

We in return will play our part in mediating for the peace and security of all the people of this Land, both Israeli and Palestinian.

> *Signed,*
> The Patriarchs, Archbishops, and Heads of all the Christian
> Churches in Jerusalem[19]

Easter Message 2002

During this sacred season, we urgently exhort all of our Christian brothers and sisters to take heart through the suffering of Christ and to work toward establishing His Kingdom where love, joy, and peace triumph. This Kingdom also requires us to echo other words that Jesus said before His death: *"Father, forgive them, for they know not what they do."*

It goes without saying that we are profoundly saddened for those who are going hungry, who are homeless, and who are without employment. We share your grief for the wounded — many of whom will be in need of long-term medical care in the future — and we offer our condolences to all those who have lost one of their loved ones.

April 2002

An Appeal for Ecumenical Prayers for Peace

[To the Israeli authorities: Lift] the closures and the curfews that are an enormous ordeal for thousands of people. . . . We are convinced that only God can deliver us from this intolerable situation. So we call upon all of the faithful in this land to join with us to intensify our prayers for peace, justice, and reconciliation. We hope that our Muslim and Jewish friends will also join their prayers with ours.[20]

August 2002

Christmas Message 2002

Christmas has come once again amidst difficulties and suffering: military occupation, curfews, harrowing daily life, and a growing hate within our hearts. It seems as if the hope of a better future is lost.[21] Nonetheless, the message of Christmas is still a message of hope, love, and peace, as well as one of justice, freedom, and security. . . . For these reasons, resist the feelings of death and discouragement, and fill your hearts and homes with the joy of Christmas: in fact, the best means by which you can stand up to the death and oppression you are being forced to endure is by keeping your joy and courage.

December 2002

FOUR

Post-Oslo

Dividing Walls of Hostility (2003-2008)

Between Palestinians and Israelis

On 16 June 2002, once again in violation of international law,[1] Israel began
to build a separation wall.[2] The construction is overwhelming confirmation of the overarching Israeli policy of "separation" from Palestinians.[3]
Palestinian human-rights lawyer Jonathan Kuttab clarifies: "This [policy]
is built on keeping people apart, not only keeping Palestinians apart from
Israelis, but fragmenting the Palestinian community into little enclaves,
each separate and divided from the other."[4] The most devastating consequences of the separation wall are felt in Jerusalem, a city whose borders,
contours, and Palestinian population have already been devastated by the
1967 occupation[5] and the 1993 closure. Palestinians with West Bank identity cards and without special permits are not allowed to visit Jerusalem for
medical care, religious services, employment, education, or family visits.
Occupied land is being annexed and confiscated, often for the accelerated
building of illegal Israeli settlements inside and outside Jerusalem municipal borders.[6] The increasing isolation of the city from its surroundings un-
dercuts any possibility that Jerusalem will be the capital of a Palestinian
state.

On 26 August 2003, faced with the fact of the Wall, the Jerusalem
Heads of Churches declared, ". . . we believe that the wall of separation
constitutes a serious obstacle [to the road map[7] to peace]. For the two nations, this wall of separation nurtures a feeling of isolation."[8] The Heads of

Churches go on to specify the effects of the Wall on Palestinians: the threat to the possibility of having a sovereign state; the inaccessibility or confiscation of their land; the further constriction on freedom of movement. They also name the Wall's peculiar psychological impact for Christians living in the place of the birth of Jesus. A year later, in their 2004 Christmas statement, the Jerusalem Heads of Churches put the effect of the Wall in still starker terms: "In these days, just before Christmas, the city [of Bethlehem] is transformed into a giant prison.[9] . . . Many of the Christian families have left Bethlehem because of the difficulties they encounter, because of the building of the 'wall of separation' and its unbelievable construction at the very entry to the city. Moreover, for this construction, much land of Christian families has been confiscated."[10] This strong sentiment is again expressed in the 2005 Christmas statement.[11]

At this time there was also strain between the Greek Orthodox Church and the Israeli government. Patriarch Ireneos I, consecrated 19 December 2001, was deposed by action of the Brotherhood of the Holy Sepulchre on 6 May 2005, an action confirmed by the Pan Orthodox Synod meeting in Istanbul on 24 May 2005. The reason for his ouster was a real-estate deal in which the Patriarch leased or sold properties near the Jaffa Gate — among these properties were the Petra building and the Imperial Hotel — to extreme right-wing Israeli settlers. The Israeli government neither recognized the ouster nor the newly elected successor to Ireneos I, Theophilos III. It is a sixteen-year-old tradition for the Greek Orthodox Patriarch of Jerusalem to be approved or recognized by the local government. Ignoring this tradition, the Israeli government stated this was "an internal church dispute." The dispute continued into 2006, when the Israeli government reiterated it would not "interfere in internal church matters."[12]

In March 2006, the Jerusalem Heads of Churches issued a statement to congratulate the newly elected Kadima[13] government, led by Ariel Sharon. Having offered congratulations, however, they chastised the Israeli government for failing to relate directly to democratically elected Palestinian leadership, and for unilateral decisions regarding the West Bank and Gaza.[14] Regarding Israeli citizens, in contrast, the Jerusalem Heads of Churches called on Palestinians to send a clear message of peace, concluding, "We are persuaded that the vast majority of both Israelis and Palestinians are tired of conflict and want to live in security, with peace and justice."[15]

A few months later, however, the statement published by the Jerusalem Heads of Churches on 7 July was once again charged by alarm: "The vio-

lence and aggression of this present moment is without proportion or justification." Among the violent incidents named were the abduction of an
Israeli soldier, the kidnapping and killing of a Jewish settler, the destruction of bridges and power substations by the IDF, which left hundreds of
thousands in Gaza without electricity and water, the abduction of seven
Palestinian cabinet ministers and twenty-one legislative council members
by the IDF, and the killing of twenty-seven civilian Palestinians in one
week. The Jerusalem Heads of Churches sounded a clarion call to bring
down the dividing wall of hostility between Israeli and Palestinian:

> Our sufferings, Israelis and Palestinians, will have an end when the truth
> on both sides is recognized. The right for Israel to have security must be
> recognized. At the same time, it must be recognized that the core of the
> conflict between Israelis and Palestinians is the deprivation of the Pales-
> tinian people of its freedom. We firmly support fighting against terror-
> ism, but we remind firmly that this fighting starts by eradicating the
> roots of all violence, which is the deprivation of the Palestinian people
> of its freedom. . . . Things have gone too far.

Once again, they called upon the international community "to intervene
and insist on a diplomatic solution to this conflict. All Authorities must
change course, and with unflinching International pressure and presence,
they have to negotiate in order to reach the just and definitive peace."

Between Palestinians

In the months following the 25 January 2006 election victory of Hamas,
another wall of hostility — at least as divisive — arose: the wall between
Fatah and Hamas. Although there had been violence between these two
factions since the early 1990s, immediately after the 2006 election and into
the autumn, Palestinian-against-Palestinian violence gathered momen-
tum. "By the end of 2006, dozens were dying each month. Some of the victims were noncombatants."[16]

On 31 January 2006, the Jerusalem Heads of Churches had issued a
congratulatory statement to the entire Palestinian people "for their democratic performance in the recent parliamentary elections." They also called
upon the Palestinian people "to continue their contribution to the making

of their history whatever may be the difficulties or obstacles, internal or external. We pray for all those who will govern in this difficult period, and we extend our cooperation to them for the public good and the national Palestinian aspirations together with the cause of justice and peace in a nonviolent way. . . ."[17]

A year later, however, in January 2007, the Jerusalem Heads of Churches issued "A Message of Concern to All the Palestinian People":

> As Leaders of the Christian Churches in Jerusalem concerned at the present situation in the Palestinian Territories, we feel we must voice our anxiety for all our people — Christian and Muslim alike — in the deteriorating relations between Fatah and Hamas leaders and the armed forces. It would appear that all kinds of mediation and attempts at reconciliation have so far failed, resulting in a deadlock in the situation. The latest allegations and threats which have been aired through the local and international media have resulted in some large-scale fighting which soon will be very difficult to stop. Added to this, the threatening language of the last few days by representatives of both movements and other related parties [is] both unprecedented and very aggressive. Such occurrences can only bring a civil war nearer by the hour.

Again, in June 2007, on the occasion of the Fortieth Anniversary of the Occupation, this statement was issued: "How painful and awful then that now we have to say stop all domestic fighting. The fighting has struck at the most vulnerable [time], thus diverting International attention away from the National issue with its priorities and so disappointing the Palestinian people's hope of attaining independence together with freedom from Occupation with its related aspects."

Palestinian lawyer, activist, and writer Raja Shehadeh identifies the roots of this internecine conflict — this "polarization of Palestinian society" — in the Oslo Accords: "Throughout the first Intifada I had felt such oneness with everyone. We were all working together for a common cause, the end of the Israeli occupation. It matters little that one was the employer and one the employee. There was a strong sense of solidarity among us. . . . Now the false peace of Oslo had divided us. . . . The false peace had shattered us like pieces of that old pot."[18]

Between Palestinians and the International Community

A third dividing wall — a wall between Palestinians and the international community — is perhaps the most confounding. Appeals to the international community for support — financial and diplomatic — appear again and again in the statements of the Jerusalem Heads of Churches, from January 1988 onward.[19] This dividing wall has been long in the making. But the January 2006 election made more acute its effect on the lives of Palestinians, since after the election many countries decided to cut off aid to the Palestinian people in an attempt to isolate and undermine the newly elected Hamas government.[20]

In May 2006, the Heads of Churches in Jerusalem sent a letter to the Heads of State, Presidents, and Prime Ministers of the European Union, the United States, and other donor countries, including Canada, Japan, and Australia, and asked them to end the boycott:

> After all, your own International Observers declared the elections to be conducted in a just and honest manner and the outcome the wish of the greater number of the Electorate. . . . More than this, we would ask that you seriously consider the potential for change which you might influence if you resolved to work with the Authority. Consultation has the possibility of encouraging efforts for good government and the abandonment of acts of terrorism. . . .

The growing divide between Palestinians and the international community is also indicated by a statement on Christian Zionism. A 22 August 2006 statement by the Jerusalem Heads of Churches resounds themes of their 25 April 1988 statement against "the so-called 'Christian Embassy.'" Two points particularly distinguish the latter statement, "The Jerusalem Declaration on Christian Zionism." This is the first point:

> Christian Zionism is . . . detrimental to a just peace within Palestine and Israel. The Christian Zionist program provides a worldview where the Gospel is identified with the ideology of empire, colonialism, and militarism. In its extreme form, it places an emphasis on apocalyptic events leading to the end of history rather than living Christ's love and justice today. We categorically reject Christian Zionist doctrines as false teaching that corrupts the biblical message of love, justice, and reconciliation.

A second point clarifies the way in which Christian Zionism, and the International Christian Embassy in Jerusalem in particular, have bolstered a dividing wall between Palestinians and the international community:

> We further reject the contemporary alliance of Christian Zionist leaders and organizations with elements in the governments of Israel and the United States that are presently imposing their unilateral pre-emptive borders and domination over Palestine. This inevitably leads to unending cycles of violence that undermine the security of all peoples of the Middle East and the rest of the world.

That is to say, the ICEJ presents itself as the Christian presence in the Holy Land, inviting governments, and the international community at large, to overlook local Christian churches and communities. This dynamic creates concrete concern that while freedom of worship and access to the Holy Places will continue to be allowed to pilgrims, the free access of local Christians may be at risk.

Freedom of access to the Holy Places is most at risk relative to Jerusalem. As already noted, Palestinian Christians who have West Bank identity cards and who do not have special permits are not allowed to enter Jerusalem. It is significant, then, that the Jerusalem Heads of Churches published a second statement on the significance of Jerusalem for Christians. The September 2006 statement does not really break new ground; it reiterates many themes of its predecessor, the November 1994 statement. This second statement is nonetheless significant simply because it was published, and published precisely at the time when the now nearly completed separation wall and the Jerusalem Envelope — that is, a complete ring of settlements around Greater Jerusalem — effectively cut the city off from Palestinian life.

In September 1996 the Heads of Churches said that Jerusalem is "the heart of the conflict and the key to peace" in the sense of "the peaceful coexistence between two peoples . . . and three faiths." Ten years later, they began with a lament: "Once more, we have experienced another period of deadly violence in the war in South Lebanon. We still face more death and demolition in Gaza, and more insecurity in the Israeli society. . . . We say it is high time to start a serious effort from all parts for a total definitive and just peace." The Jerusalem Heads of Churches then reissue a call: ". . . we believe that peace must begin in this Holy City of Jerusalem."

The 2006 statement also addressed the changed reality since 1994: "With the construction of the wall, many of our faithful are excluded from the precincts of the Holy City, and according to plans published in the local press, many more will also be excluded in the future. Surrounded by walls, Jerusalem is no longer at the center and is no longer the heart of life as she should be." The strategy, declared the Heads of Churches, must be

> a concerted effort to search for a common vision on the status of this Holy City based on international resolutions and having regard to the rights of two peoples in her and the three faith communities. . . . In God's own design, two peoples and three religions have been living together in this city. Our vision is that they should continue to live together in harmony, respect, mutual acceptance, and cooperation.

Still, the Jerusalem Heads of Churches are clear: the vision of security, freedom, justice, and peace will be realized only if and as the international community is willing to be engaged and to exert pressure on Israel to abide by international law. This is indeed the heartbeat of their twenty-year testament.

The Jerusalem Heads of Churches Speak

26 August 2003–22 January 2008

Statement regarding the Separation Wall

We, the Heads of Churches in Jerusalem, affirm our determination to do all in our power to work for Peace in this Holy Land — a Peace that is concerned with the well-being of every resident of this Land, be they Israeli or Palestinian, to give them security, justice, freedom, independence, and personal dignity.

Let no one doubt our abhorrence of violence, whoever the perpetrator. Peace will only be established when all violence is eradicated from both sides. If the present Road Map for Peace is to bring positive results, we believe the Separation Wall constitutes a grave obstacle. For both nations the Wall will result in a feeling of isolation.[21] Moreover, for many Palestinians it means the deprivation of land (some 10% more than that of the Occupation in 1967), livelihood, statehood, and family life. Occupation remains the root cause of the conflict and of the continuing suffering in the Holy Land.

Take, for example, the proposed[22] Separation Wall around Bethlehem, for us Christians, the birthplace of Jesus Christ, the Prince of Peace. The consequences will be devastating to the Christian Community; not least the psychological impact on daily life. The community will be isolated following the deprivation of access to land and freedom of movement. Visits of pilgrims will be further discouraged.

We appeal to both Authorities — Israeli and Palestinian — and to all

Peace-loving peoples around the world (who should make urgent contact with their leaders, both political and religious) — in an effort to remove this impediment to a comprehensive and lasting Peace.

Jerusalem, 26th August 2003

Signed by
+ Patriarch Michel Sabbah
  Latin Patriarch of Jerusalem
+ Patriarch Torkom II
  Armenian Apostolic Orthodox Patriarch of Jerusalem
  Fr. Giovanni Battistelli, O.F.M.
  Custos of the Holy Land
+ Anba Abraham
  Coptic Orthodox Archbishop of Jerusalem
+ Swerios Malki Murad
  Syrian Orthodox Archbishop of Jerusalem
+ Abba Cuostos
  Ethiopian Orthodox Archbishop of Jerusalem
+ Riah Abu El-Assal
  Anglican Bishop in Jerusalem
+ Munib A. Younan
  Lutheran Evangelical Bishop of Jerusalem
  Archimandrite Mtanious Haddad
  Greek Catholic Patriarchal Exarch in Jerusalem
+ Butros Malki
  Syrian Catholic Bishop in Jerusalem

Christmas Message 2004

We went to Bethlehem to celebrate the mystery of Christmas, in spite of the grave difficulties our people are living through, including the recent death of President Yasser Arafat.[23] Our lives are still filled with a deep sense of despair, made more so by the dramatic climb in unemployment and in poverty. There is still no justice or peace. Blood is being shed and political prisoners are detained in their prisons. The two people of this Holy Land are still in the quest for peace and justice, grappling to come to terms with the hostilities, the murders, and the blood that has been spilled in Palestine and in Israel. . . .[24]

The future of Bethlehem itself demands special attention. Surely you will sing Christmas carols evoking imagery of "the little town of Bethlehem." This little town has particular need for support in order to remain the town of peace where those who believe in Jesus the Savior and the Prince of Peace can dwell. In these days just before Christmas, the town has been transformed into a large prison and the construction of "The Wall" around it continues. Many Christian families have already left Bethlehem because of the difficulties they have encountered, due to the building of this "wall of separation" and the unbelievable construction at the entrance to the town. All this work has also led to the confiscation of land from many Christian families.

However, at the present time we see small signs of hope: promises that soon some of the political prisoners will be freed by the Israelis and hopes for the renewal of efforts on all sides with a view towards the implementation of peace accords. . . .

The Churches of the world are called upon to remember that the Holy Land is the land of the roots of all Christians. This is why every believer and every church has a duty to pay special attention to the events that are unfolding in this land, and to lead a well-coordinated, worldwide movement to help the two peoples find reconciliation based on security, justice, and equality for all in their rights, duties, and the dignity given by God to each and every one of them.

As the leaders of the Churches, we will pursue our efforts to construct bridges of peace and hope by raising our voices for justice for all people. . . . We pray and hope that the days are coming when the residents of Bethlehem and of all the Holy Land may live in freedom without the need for a wall of security and separation.

December 2004

Christmas Message 2005

As we prepare ourselves to celebrate yet another Christmastide, let us pause a moment in prayer and meditation, and get a handle on the reality of our country. When we look at our Holy Land, we still see the will to war within the souls of many people, and therefore we are seeing continual violence, assassinations, and arrests as well as the pursuit of the construction of this wall, the consolidation of the barriers between two peoples and a rise in the fear and the hate in their hearts. However, there are also several positive signs: the decision of the Palestinian Authority to say no to the violence and to adopt only peaceful means of arriving at peace and justice; and corresponding positive signs are manifesting themselves in the Israeli leadership, who appear to be joining with the will of the Palestinians, in their new decision to leave this long conflict behind in order to obtain security, justice, peace, and the beginning of a new life for the two peoples of this Holy Land.

December 2005

The Patriarchs and Heads of the Churches of Jerusalem

The Palestinian Election

01-Feb-06

Latin Patriarchate of Jerusalem

We congratulate the Palestinian people for their democratic performance in the recent parliamentary elections. We express our respect and our support to the will of the people expressed in these elections. We congratulate all those who were elected.

Our message as Christian leaders in this new phase of our history is the message of our faith and our concern for all. Some may be afraid or troubled because of this new phase. We respond, first, with the words of Jesus Christ: "Do not let your hearts be troubled or afraid. Peace I bequeath to you; my peace I give you, a peace which the world cannot give" (Jn.

14:27). Second, "Be strong and stand firm" (Josh. 1:9). We call upon the Palestinian people to continue their contribution to the making of their history whatever may be the difficulties or obstacles, internal or external. We pray for all those who will govern in this difficult period, and we extend our cooperation to them for the public good and the national Palestinian aspirations together with the cause of justice and peace in a nonviolent way, whether in regard to foreign relations, [or] the rule of law together with full religious freedom, especially in the social and educational fields.

Our message to the Government of Hamas, members and leadership, is the message of Our Lord Jesus Christ in his Sermon on the Mountain: "Blessed are the poor in spirit: the kingdom of heaven is theirs. Blessed are the gentle: they shall have the earth as their inheritance. Blessed are those who mourn: they shall be comforted. Blessed are those who hunger and thirst for uprightness: they shall have their fill. Blessed are the merciful: they shall have mercy shown them. Blessed are the pure in heart: they shall see God. Blessed are the peacemakers: they shall be recognized as children of God" (Mt. 5:3-10).

We ask God to guide us towards what is good for all and for this Holy Land and its inhabitants, Palestinians and Israelis, be they Moslems, Christians, or Jews.

+ Patriarch Theophilos III: Greek Orthodox Patriarchate
+ Patriarch Michel Sabbah: Latin Patriarchate
+ Patriarch Torkom II: Armenian Apostolic Orthodox Patriarchate
  Father Pierbattista Pizzaballa, O.F.M., Custos of the Holy Land
+ Anba Abraham: Coptic Orthodox Patriarchate
+ Swerios Malki Mourad: Syrian Orthodox Patriarchate
+ Abune Grima: Ethiopian Orthodox Patriarchate
+ Paul Nabil Sayyah: Maronite Patriarchal Exarchate
+ Bishop Riah Abu El-Assal: Episcopal Church of Jerusalem and the
    Middle East
+ Bishop Mounib Younan: Lutheran Evangelical Church
+ Pierre Melki, Exarch for the Syrian Catholics — Jerusalem
+ Andre Dikran Bedoghlyan: Armenian Catholic Patriarchal Exarchate
  Archimandrite Mtanious Haddad: Greek Catholic Patriarchal
    Exarchate

Church Leaders in Jerusalem Urge World Churches and All Christians to Advocate for Peace

"They have treated the wounds of my people lightly, saying 'Peace, peace' when there is no Peace." Jeremiah 6:14

"If one member suffers, all members suffer with it." 1 Corinthians 12:26

"Make plain the vision." Habakkuk 2:2

Churches and Christian brothers and sisters around the world:
Grace and Peace to you from Jerusalem,

The World Council of Churches together with Churches and international agencies have joined together for a special Christian advocacy initiative called International Church Action for Peace in Palestine and Israel, March 12-19, 2006. This initiative comes from those who are part of the Ecumenical Accompaniment Program in Palestine and Israel (EAPPI) together with Pax Christi International. The EAPPI began three years ago as a response to a call from the Churches in Jerusalem. Today, one year away from the fortieth anniversary of the illegal Israeli Occupation of Palestine, we renew our call and urge you to actively participate in the worldwide week of Christian advocacy for a just peace.

During the last thirty-nine years, Churches, Church Leaders, and ordinary Christians have worked tirelessly and patiently advocating for peace in Palestine and Israel. Now, as the situation continues to deteriorate and opportunities for peace are forsaken, it is crucial for Christians to make their voices heard vigorously in the public arena. Together with the strong and deeply treasured actions of prayer and Christian solidarity, the Churches in Jerusalem and the Holy Land need you to speak with the moral authority of the church from the ethical perspective of the Christian faith. Lawmakers and politicians in your country need to know that the Churches are well aware of the ongoing suffering caused by the Occupation and the subsequent insecurity and are becoming even more actively involved in seeking a just peace. All national governments have a responsibility to uphold international law, and Christians have a role in holding our governments to account.

We ask all Christians to consider the prophetic role of the Church and the power and importance of public witness so that the sufferings, injustices, and insecurity of the Occupation, which affects Israelis and Palestinians — be they Christians, Muslims, or Jews — becomes an urgent priority for all national governments.

The positive attention given to the unilateral pullout from the Gaza Strip has served to draw world attention away from the realities on the West Bank and East Jerusalem. There is a steady expansion of Israeli military control. Settler blocs continue to grow and land is illegally seized to build a wall which has been condemned internationally. West Bank cities are being choked to death economically, and the people live in constant fear of military incursions. The security situation within the Palestinian Territories is in crisis, and the Palestinian Authority must be supported in their efforts to impose the rule of law and at the same time be held accountable in fulfilling their responsibilities.

The price of Occupation is unbearably high for those living in Israel as well. The country is dominated by insecurity, fear, and poverty at the same time social inequalities spiral out of control.

Palestinian Christians face the same struggles and suffer the same desperate situation as all other Palestinians, but we also face an alarming rate of migration out of Palestine. The Christian presence in Palestine is important for the whole society, and we are concerned for the future of our community and for the institutions that serve all Palestinians.

The same solution is required to end the suffering in both Israel and Palestine: a just peace reached through negotiations guided by international law. An end to the illegal Occupation is the first step towards real peace and security for both Israel and Palestine. Peace, Justice, and Security for Palestine will bring Peace, Justice, and Security for Israel.

We continue to pray for the peace of Jerusalem and to insist that a shared and open Jerusalem, which respects the rights and sovereignty of the three religions and two peoples, is essential to a just peace in the Middle East.

The Christian perspective on law and justice leads us to call for a two-state solution based on international law which provides a truly viable, contiguous, independent, sovereign state.

We affirm a vision of Peace with Justice based on reconciliation. We as

Christians have faith in God's power and presence. Our faith is a well-spring of hope and perseverance. It is that very hope that leads us to assert that the present situation can and must be changed. We call for assertive, non-violent efforts to bring peace, and we condemn in the strongest possible terms all those that use violence and acts of terror.

However, the situation is urgent.[25] With every passing month the possibility of a peaceful negotiated solution grows more distant. The more settlements that are built and the more the Wall sets the borders on confiscated lands means that the West Bank communities are separated further from each other.[26] Similarly, as Muslims and Christians have further restrictions on access to the Holy Sites, especially in Jerusalem, the people cannot travel, and families are separated. Palestinian children are illegally detained, and more Palestinian Christians leave the Holy Land because of lack of work, security, and hope for the future. In consequence, a viable, contiguous Palestinian State becomes less likely. Every day is pushing a short-term solution further away.

We hope and pray that Christians throughout the world will join together in the week of March 12 to 19 to make a public witness for peace. It is our prayer that you will speak boldly to your lawmakers to lift up the suffering of the people and to ask them to undertake specific actions for peace.

In Jerusalem, Bethlehem, and Ramallah, Christians will be gathering in joint services on March 12 to launch the International Church Action for Peace in Palestine and Israel and lift up the Christian voice for a Just Peace. Join us in your own country and speak to your own government.

It is your solidarity that together with God's grace helps us to be advocates of Peace and ministers of Reconciliation in this war-torn place. God has given us the vision of Peace with Justice: Join with us to "make plain the vision."

Patriarchs and Heads of Churches in Jerusalem, 06-02-2006

To the Newly Elected Kadima Party Leadership

On this occasion we would like to express our concern on the matter of all that has been said about Israeli intentions to proceed with the implementation of unilateral measures against the West Bank, while apparently circumventing the Palestinians and their democratically elected leadership.

We urge the Israeli Leadership to demonstrate their courage and their wisdom in resuming the peace process with the Palestinians. At the same time, we likewise urge the Palestinians to send a clear message of peace to Israeli citizens. We are convinced that the great majority of Israelis and Palestinians are weary of conflict and desirous of living in security, peace, and justice.

The international community is being called upon to make it clear to all parties — but especially to those who have the power to make decisions in Israel, who for the moment hold the major decision-making power in the Holy Land — that unilateral measures would probably bring about some temporary solutions, but would not put an end to the mistrust and the mutual misunderstanding shared by the two peoples living in this blessed and beloved land.

In our role as Christian leaders we are resolved to do all that is in our power to promote peace, mutual understanding, and justice for all, and we hope to see a similar commitment from the Islamic and Judaic leadership.

29 March 2006

Easter Message 2006

We know that our lives in this land are frustrating and filled with hardships. Nowadays it seems as if we either confront uncharted waters or come to an impasse in the world of politics between the new Israeli and the new Palestinian governments. In the first instance we are making an appeal to the international community, which has decided to boycott the Palestinian people:[27] it is unacceptable to boycott a people on whom oppression and injustice have been and continue to be imposed, while that community, up to this point, has remained unresponsive in putting an end to the humiliation of human beings. Instead of boycotting, we call upon the international community to seize the opportunity at this stage of the history of this conflict to seriously attempt to put an end to the suffering of our land and all its inhabitants. . . .

We make the same appeal to our leaders, knowing that they are facing some difficult decisions. Where there is a sincere will, there is the possibility and the strength to surmount all obstacles so as to achieve security, peace, and justice for all, Palestinians and Israelis alike. We make the same appeal to the Israeli authorities, so that they would see that unilateral measures would only add to the conflict and the continual suffering of the two peoples. This is why we urge them to take just measures to free the Israeli human and the Palestinian human, and to see in the Palestinian Authority a helper and a partner in the building of a peace whose accomplishment is not impossible.

We would like to greet our brothers and sisters around the world, wishing them all a truly Blessed Easter. You are also called upon to be witnesses of the Risen Jesus. You, along with us, bear the responsibility of bringing about a reconciliation in this Holy Land, a reconciliation based on truth, justice, and equality among persons and among peoples. We are grateful for all your efforts and for your solidarity. But we ask that you take a moment with us, in this Holy Week, to ponder the mystery of love contained in this sacred time and ask yourselves: Have we done all that we could have done to bring justice and human dignity to the human beings and to the believers who live around the Holy Places, wherein lie the roots of our faith and of the Redemption of the world? Ask of your governments: Are you incapable of stopping the suffering of the two peoples in this land? Ask of the media in your countries: In all that you report, is it your goal to bring life, love, and trust between the two peoples of this land? Question them, and question yourselves as well, about this so-called "Security/Separation Wall," about the numerous blockades and checkpoints and about the trampled dignity of the human being in the land of Redemption and love.

April 2006

To the Heads of State — Presidents/Prime Ministers of the EU, USA, and other donor countries incl. Canada, Japan, Australia, etc.

Your Excellencies,

We greet you in the name of Peace and Justice from the Holy City of Jerusalem!

As Heads of Churches we are very much concerned for the well-being of our people, who are now faced with even greater hardships if your countries persist in their decision to cut off the aid to the Palestinian people and isolate the newly elected Palestinian Authority.

In God's name we would urge you to re-consider your decision. After all, your own International Observers declared the elections to be conducted in a just and honest manner and the outcome the wish of the greater number of the Electorate — hopeful of gaining an improvement in their daily lives through a more accountable Authority.

More than this, we would ask that you seriously consider the potential for change which you might influence if you resolved to work with the Authority. Consultation has the possibility of encouraging efforts for good government and the abandonment of acts of terrorism; in the present volatile situation neglect of such an opportunity could lead to an even worse scenario.

We much appreciate the assistance given to Church Institutions — particularly schools and hospitals — where we are struggling to ensure their continuing work to some 25% of Palestinian society. However, we strongly oppose any attempt to set parallel funding mechanisms.

In conclusion, we would seek your support for our work as peacemakers and carers whilst pleading that you ensure that the demands of international law be upheld equally for Israel and the Palestinians. We condemn acts of violence and terrorism regardless of the perpetrators.

Patriarchs and Heads of Churches in Jerusalem

May 2006

Statement of Heads of Churches

Stop All the Violence, Pursue a Just Peace

> *"Justice is turned back, and righteousness stands at a distance; for truth stumbles from the public square, and uprightness cannot enter. Truth is lacking, and whoever turns from evil is despoiled. The Lord saw it, and it displeased him that there was no justice. He saw that there was no one, and was appalled that there was no one to intervene" (Isaiah 59:14-16).*

The violence and aggression of this present moment [are] without proportion or justification.

An Israeli soldier was taken prisoner in combat. A Jewish settler was kidnapped and killed. As Israeli response, three bridges were destroyed and a power substation was disabled, causing tens of millions of dollars of damage and leaving up to 750,000 people without electricity or water in Gaza. Moreover, the Israeli forces have abducted 84 persons, among them 7 Cabinet Ministers and 21 members of the Palestinian Legislative Council. This comes after a week in which 48 Palestinians were killed and among the dead were 27 innocent civilians, including nine children and a pregnant woman.

Today, we Christian Heads of the Churches in Jerusalem, we say: It is against law and reason what is still happening in our land. It is our duty as religious leaders to keep saying this to the Authorities. It is against law and reason that you remain, and you keep us on the ways of death. *"The Lord saw it, and it displeased him that there was no justice. He saw that there was no one, and was appalled that there was no one to intervene" (Isaiah 59:16).*

We condemn the abduction of the Israeli soldier, the killing of the settler youth, as we condemn the daily abduction and killing of tens of Palestinians as well as the keeping of thousands of them in prisons. All human beings, Israelis and Palestinians, have the same dignity and must be equally treated. All aggression against human dignity, whether Israeli or Palestinian, must stop.

Our sufferings, Israelis and Palestinians, will have an end when the truth on both sides is recognized. The right for Israel to have security must be recognized. At the same time, it must be recognized that the core of the conflict between Israelis and Palestinians is the deprivation of the Palestinian people of its freedom. We firmly support fighting against terrorism, but we remind firmly that this fighting starts by eradicating the roots of all violence, which is the deprivation of the Palestinian people of its freedom.

It is against law and reason to keep going in the way of death. The moral imperative is clear. Stop all the violence. Stop the killing. Protect the life and dignity of the people. Begin negotiations. Break this murderous chain of violence in which we are ensnared. And listen to God's call: *"De-part from evil and do good; seek peace and pursue it" (Psalm 3[4]:1[4])*.

Things have gone too far. We call on the International community to intervene and insist on a diplomatic solution to this conflict. All Author-ities must change course, and with unflinching International pressure and presence, they have to negotiate in order to reach the just and definitive peace. *"What does the Lord require of you [but] to do justice, love kindness, and walk humbly with your God?" (Micah 6:8)*.

+ Patriarch Theophilos III: Greek Orthodox Patriarchate
+ Patriarch Michel Sabbah: Latin Patriarchate
+ Patriarch Torkom II: Armenian Apostolic Orthodox Patriarchate
  Rev. Pierbattista Pizzaballa, O.F.M., Custos of the Holy Land
+ Anba Abraham: Coptic Orthodox Patriarchate
+ Abune Grima: Ethiopian Orthodox Patriarchate
+ Paul Nabil Sayyah: Maronite Patriarchal Exarchate
+ Bishop Riah Abu Al-Assal: Episcopal Church of Jerusalem and the
    Middle East
+ Bishop Mounib Younan: Lutheran Evangelical Church
+ Pierre Malki: Exarch for the Syrian Catholics — Jerusalem
+ George Baker: Greek Catholic Patriarchal Exarchate
  Rev. Rafael Minassian: Armenian Catholic Patriarchal Exarchate

Jerusalem, 7 July 2006

The Jerusalem Declaration on Christian Zionism

"We stand for Justice. We can do no other."

"Blessed are the peacemakers, for they shall be called the children of God" (Matthew 5:9).

Christian Zionism is a modern theological and political movement that embraces the most extreme ideological positions of Zionism, thereby becoming detrimental to a just peace within Palestine and Israel.

The Christian Zionist program provides a worldview where the Gospel is identified with the ideology of empire, colonialism, and militarism. In its extreme form, it places an emphasis on apocalyptic events leading to the end of history rather than living Christ's love and justice today.

We categorically reject Christian Zionist doctrines as false teaching that corrupts the biblical message of love, justice, and reconciliation.

We further reject the contemporary alliance of Christian Zionist leaders and organizations with elements in the governments of Israel and the United States that are presently imposing their unilateral pre-emptive borders and domination over Palestine.

This inevitably leads to unending cycles of violence that undermine the security of all peoples of the Middle East and the rest of the world.

We reject the teachings of Christian Zionism that facilitate and support these policies as they advance racial exclusivity and perpetual war rather than the gospel of universal love, redemption, and reconciliation taught by Jesus Christ.

Rather than condemn the world to the doom of Armageddon we call upon everyone to liberate themselves from the ideologies of militarism and occupation. Instead, let them pursue the healing of the nations!

We call upon Christians in churches on every continent to pray for the Palestinian and Israeli people, both of whom are suffering as victims of occupation and militarism.

These discriminative actions are turning Palestine into impoverished ghettos surrounded by exclusive Israeli settlements.

The establishment of the illegal settlements and the construction of the Separation Wall on confiscated Palestinian land undermine the viability of a Palestinian state as well as peace and security in the entire region.

We call upon all churches that remain silent to break their silence and speak for reconciliation with justice in the Holy Land.[28]

Therefore, we commit ourselves to the following principles as an alternative way:

We affirm that all people are created in the image of God. In turn they are called to honor the dignity of every human being and to respect their inalienable rights.

We affirm that Israelis and Palestinians are capable of living together within peace, justice, and security.

We affirm that Palestinians are one people, both Muslim and Christian. We reject all attempts to subvert and fragment their unity.

We call upon all people to reject the narrow worldview of Christian Zionism and other ideologies that privilege one people at the expense of others.

We are committed to non-violent resistance as the most effective means to end the illegal occupation in order to attain a just and lasting peace.

With urgency we warn that Christian Zionism and its alliances are justifying colonization, apartheid, and empire-building.

God demands that justice be done. No enduring peace, security, or reconciliation is possible without the foundation of justice. The demands of justice will not disappear. The struggle for justice must be pursued diligently and persistently but without violence.

"What does the Lord require of you: To act justly, to love mercy, and to walk humbly with your God" (Micah 6:8).

This is where we take our stand. We stand for justice. We can do no other. Justice alone guarantees a peace that will lead to reconciliation with a life of security and prosperity for all the peoples of our land. By standing on the side of justice, we open ourselves to the work of peace — and working for peace makes us children of God.

"God was reconciling the world to himself in Christ, not counting men's sins against them. And he has committed to us the message of reconciliation" (2 Corinthians 5:19).

Patriarch Michel Sabbah, Latin Patriarchate, Jerusalem
Archbishop Swerios Malki Mourad, Syrian Orthodox Patriarchate, Jerusalem
Bishop Riah Abu El-Assal, Episcopal Church of Jerusalem and the Middle East
Bishop Munib Younan, Evangelical Lutheran Church in Jordan and the Holy Land

22 August 2006

Patriarchs and Heads of the Local Christian Churches in Jerusalem

Status of Jerusalem

September 29, 2006

Once more, we have experienced another period of deadly violence in the war in South Lebanon.[29] We still face more death and demolition in Gaza, and more insecurity in the Israeli society. Therefore, we say it is high time to start a serious effort from all parts for a total definitive and just peace. Moreover, we believe that peace must begin in this Holy City of Jerusalem.

Therefore, we present the following statement, hoping it will bring a modest contribution to the birth of peace in our Land.

In 1994, we, the patriarchs and heads of the local Christian Churches in Jerusalem, published a memorandum entitled "The Meaning of Jerusalem for Christians" that insisted on the Christian character of Jerusalem, and on the importance of the Christian presence in her.

It also discussed the special political status that must be accorded to the city because of her sacred character. Since that time, we have witnessed the increasing tendency of the political authorities to unilaterally decide the fate of the city and define her status. The access of our faithful and our personnel to Jerusalem is ever more difficult.

With the construction of the wall, many of our faithful are excluded from the precincts of the Holy City, and according to plans published in the local press, many more will also be excluded in the future. Surrounded by walls, Jerusalem is no longer the center and is no longer the heart of life as she should be.

We consider it part of our duty to draw the attention of the local authorities, as well as the international community and the world churches, to this very grave situation and call for a concerted effort to search for a common vision on the status of this Holy City based on international resolutions and having regard to the rights of two peoples in her and the three faith communities.

In this city, in which God chose to speak to humanity and to reconcile peoples with himself and among themselves, we raise our voices to say that the paths, followed up till now, have not brought about the pacification of the city and have not reassured normal life for her inhabitants. Therefore they must be changed. The political leaders must search for a new vision as well as for new means.

In God's own design, two peoples and three religions have been living together in this city. Our vision is that they should continue to live together in harmony, respect, mutual acceptance, and cooperation.

1. Jerusalem, Holy City and city of daily life for two peoples and three religions

Jerusalem, heritage of humanity and Holy City, is also the city of daily life for her inhabitants, both Palestinians and Israelis, Jews, Christians, and Muslims, and for all who are linked to them by family ties as well as for those for whom Jerusalem is the location of their prayer, of their schools, hospitals, and workplaces.

Not only historical memories and sacred places of pilgrimage, but also living communities of believers, Jews, Christians, and Muslims, make the city of Jerusalem beloved and unique for each one of the three monotheistic faiths. Holy places and living human communities are inseparable.

In addition, both the sacred character of the Holy City and the needs of her inhabitants have attracted and continue to attract numerous religious institutions. These have been recognized by the successive authorities throughout the centuries and have acquired certain rights that allow them to fulfill their obligations toward the Holy City and her inhabitants.

Consequently, the fundamental rights pertaining to both individuals and institutions must be respected. For individuals, these are basic rights that permit them to exercise their religious, political, and social duties and to meet their religious, educational, cultural, and medical needs.

For communities, this is the right to possess, to freely administer the works necessary for their ministry and their overall human development — churches, monasteries, schools, hospitals, social institutions, theological and biblical institutes, accommodation for pilgrims, etc. It also includes the right to bring in the personnel and avail of the means needed for the proper functioning of the institutions.

2. Requirements for a just and durable solution for the Jerusalem question

The future of the city must be decided by common agreement, through collaboration and consultation and not imposed by power and force. Unilateral decisions or imposed solutions will continue to be very detrimental to peace and security.

Different solutions are possible. The city of Jerusalem might remain united but sovereignty in this case must be shared, exercised according to a principle of equality by both Israelis and Palestinians. However, the city might also be divided if this be the desire of the two peoples who live here, with two distinct sovereignties, the aim of which would be to reach a true unity of hearts in the two parts of the city.

The wall, which tears apart the city at more than one point and which excludes a great number of her inhabitants, must give way to an education that will strengthen mutual trust and acceptance.

Face to face with the inability of the parties involved to find a just and durable solution up until the present time, the assistance of the international community is a necessity. In the future too, this aid needs to continue in the form of guarantees that will ensure the stability of the agreements reached by the two sides.

We recommend to create, as soon as possible, an ad hoc committee to reflect on the future of the city. In this committee the local Churches of Jerusalem must be a part.

3. Special status — open city

Jerusalem, Holy City, heritage of humanity, city of two peoples and three religions, has a unique character that distinguishes her from all other cities of the world; a character which surpasses any local political sovereignty.

"Jerusalem is too precious to be dependent solely on municipal or national political authorities" (cf. Memorandum, 1994).

Jerusalem's two peoples are the guardians of her sanctity and carry a double responsibility: to organize their lives in the city and to welcome all the "pilgrims" who come from around the world. The needed international collaboration is not meant to replace the role and the sovereignty of her two peoples. It is rather needed in order to help both peoples to reach the definition and the stability of the special status of the city.

That is why, concretely, and from the political, economic and social point of view, her two peoples must bestow on Jerusalem a special status that corresponds to her double character, holy and universal, and ordinary and local, where daily life unfolds.

Once this status has been found and defined, the international community is required to confirm it with international guarantees that will assure the continuing peace and respect for all.

The components of this special status must include the following elements:

"The human right of freedom of worship and of conscience for all, both as individuals and as religious communities" (cf. Memorandum, 1994).

Equality of all her inhabitants before the law, in coordination with the international resolutions.

Free access to Jerusalem for all, citizens, residents, or pilgrims, at all times, whether in peace or in war. Therefore Jerusalem should be an open city.

The "rights of property ownership, custody, and worship which the different Churches have acquired throughout history should continue to be retained by the same communities. These rights, which are already protected in the Status Quo of the Holy Places according to historical 'firmans' and other documents, should continue to be recognized and respected" (cf. Memorandum, 1994).

The various Christian holy places in the city, wherever they are, must remain united in geography, whatever the solution envisaged.

Conclusion

For Jews, Christians, and Muslims, Jerusalem is a high place of revelation and of God's encounter with humanity. That is why we cannot remain indifferent to her fate nor remain silent in the face of her sufferings.

"For Jerusalem's sake I will not rest until her vindication shines out like the dawn and her salvation like a burning torch" (Isaiah 62:1).

We are launching this solemn appeal to all the religious leaders in the Holy Land to collaborate together in order to reach a common vision of the city that might unite the hearts of all believers. We call on our political authorities to seek out the common points of agreement and, in cooperation with the religious authorities, to find a solution which corresponds to the city's sacred character.

We hope that our appeal might be heard and that the political leaders, respecting the nature of this Holy City, might show themselves capable of reaching a final and definitive agreement that might make of Jerusalem a true sign of the presence of God and of his peace among all.

Patriarch Theophilos III: Greek Orthodox Patriarchate

Patriarch Michel Sabbah: Latin Patriarchate

Patriarch Torkom II: Armenian Apostolic Patriarchate

Father Pier Battista Pizzaballa: Custos of the Holy Land

Anba Abraham: Coptic Orthodox Patriarchate

Swerios Malki Mourad: Syrian Orthodox Patriarchate

Abune Grima: Ethiopian Orthodox Patriarchate

Paul Nabil Sayyah: Maronite Patriarchal Exarchate

Bishop Riah Abu Al-Assal: Episcopal Church of Jerusalem and the Middle East

Bishop Mounib Younan: Lutheran Evangelical Church

Pierre Malki: Exarch for the Syrian Catholics — Jerusalem

George Baker: Greek Catholic Patriarchal Exarchate

Father Rafael Minassian: Armenian Catholic Patriarchal Exarchate

A Message of Concern to All the Palestinian People

As Leaders of the Christian Churches in Jerusalem concerned at the present situation in the Palestinian Territories, we feel we must voice our anxiety for all our people — Christian and Moslem alike — at the deteriorating relations between Fatah and Hamas and the armed forces.

It would appear that all kinds of mediation and attempts at reconciliation have so far failed, resulting in a deadlock in the situation. The latest allegations and threats which have been aired through the local and international media have resulted in some large-scale fighting which soon will be very difficult to stop. Added to this, the threatening language of the last few days by representatives of both movements and other related parties [is] both unprecedented and very aggressive. Such occurrences can only bring a civil war nearer by the hour. The outcome would be so drastic that it will obscure the real priorities of the whole Palestinian issue.

So we feel the time has come to call for intense prayer to Almighty God for peace and an opportunity for calm in order that all parties can consider carefully the various issues at stake. Instead of hurling accusations at each other, we would urge everyone to pray for their neighbors in the widest possible sense. It is surely time to unite rather than collide. Fighting and kidnapping opponents will *not* bring down the Security Wall or end the embargo on the Palestinian people.

We believe we have an obligation to change course especially for the sake of all our children and young people, who deserve a better future devoid of hatred and bitterness. Bloodshed and violence will not bring peace; [they] will only further destroy family life and further endanger the economy of our land.

The time has come for all-out effort to unite our people and to concentrate on working for Independence together with the opportunity for all the people of this Holy Land — Christian, Moslem, and Jew — to know security and peace.

We are ready to play our part in attempting to end the present situation as quickly as possible as mediators or in whatever role deemed necessary and helpful by our people. It is vital to bring a real sense of unity in government; to unite the security forces; remove arms from our streets; and encourage the Israeli and Palestinian leaders to return to the negotiating table.

In conclusion we would remind everyone of the words of our Blessed Lord:

"Blessed are the peacemakers: they shall be called children of God" **(Matt. 5:9).**

+ Patriarch Theophilos III, Greek Orthodox Patriarchate
+ Patriarch Michel Sabbah, Latin Patriarchate
+ Patriarch Torkom II, Armenian Apostolic Orthodox Patriarchate
  Fr. Pierbattista Pizzaballa, O.F.M., Custos of the Holy Land
+ Anba Abraham, Coptic Orthodox Patriarchate
+ Archbishop Swerios Malki Mourad, Syrian Orthodox Patriarchate
+ Abune Matthias, Ethiopian Orthodox Patriarchate
+ Archbishop Paul Nabil Sayyah, Maronite Patriarchal Exarchate

+ Bishop Riah Abu Al-Assal, Episcopal Church of Jerusalem and the Middle East
+ Bishop Mounib Younan, Evangelical Lutheran Church in Jordan and the Holy Land
+ Pierre Malki, Syrian Catholic Patriarchal Exarchate
+ Bishop Baker, Greek Catholic Patriarchal Exarchate
  Fr. Raphael Minassian, Armenian Catholic Patriarchal Exarchate

Easter Message 2007

The Patriarchs and Heads of Local Churches in Jerusalem

> "All I want is to know Christ and the power of His Resurrection and to share His sufferings" (Philippians 3:10).

Sisters and Brothers here and in all the world:

We greet you in the name of our Risen Lord and ask God to fill you with the joy and strength of the Resurrection.

Having opposed early Christians and, indeed, sought to bring many of them to trial for their faith, St. Paul [was] suddenly challenged by our Blessed Lord as he journeyed to Damascus. Within a short time he became a powerful messenger for Jesus. Reading his various Epistles we see he has much to say on many aspects of the Christian faith. The statement he sets before the Philippians is regarded by many people as the most powerful: "All I want is to know Christ and the power of His Resurrection and to share His sufferings." In this short sentence he links the Cross and the Resurrection. The sufferings he has to face for his faith lead him to become conscious of the power of the Resurrection given to those who truly believe, through the power of the Holy Spirit.

Yet again, recent months have shown us much of the hardships and sufferings people have to endure, not least in this Land. Much of this burden has arisen from man's inhumanity to man together with his deprivation of basic human dignity and rights, as it happens to us because of the siege imposed upon us.

131

Our Blessed Lord challenges all of us that if we would be His disciples, we must take up our Cross and follow Him. In the midst of sufferings we reach the power of the Resurrection and the power of the Spirit that enable us to take away the oppressions that are imposed upon us.

So, as we celebrate the joy of Easter, we must examine carefully where we stand in relation to God. Many of us need to abandon the selfish instinct within us. If we would truly seek the power of the Resurrection in our lives, then we must disregard any idea we might have of self-sufficiency or worldly hopes that hide from our eyes the things of heaven and of the Spirit. If we believe in the Resurrection, we must affirm that our security is with God and in the power of the Resurrection. Again St. Paul reminds us when writing to the Corinthians: "We have this treasure. It is in earthly vessels, to show that the transcendent Power belongs to God and not to us" (2 Corinthians 4:7).

Despite our weakness and despite the unjust circumstances imposed upon us, the power of God can free us if we come to understand the logic of the Spirit in us and, if we accept [it], to behave accordingly. On the first Good Friday the disciples of Jesus doubtless felt shattered. However, gradually their faith was restored as they became conscious of their Risen Lord. Their own personal darkness of fear and uncertainty was suddenly illuminated by the light of Jesus' Resurrection.

So as we celebrate the Resurrection, we must be more diligent in searching for the light and in using it to build a better tomorrow for all of us, Palestinians or Israelis, Moslems, Jews, Christians, and Druzes.[30] We re-search for the light that comes from God, illuminates all Creation, guides every true believer in his search, and help[s] him to find God's freedom for all His people together with His peace and justice.

As we greet our sisters and brothers across the world, we wish them the joy of Easter and the power of the Risen Lord in their daily lives. Whilst conscious of the care and concern shown by many of you, we again would ask for your particular prayers for this Land, that God will guide all its governors and show them the path of justice and equality between all. Pray for the newly formed Unity Government of the Palestinians together with the Israeli Government and the Arab Initiative, to work for taking away fear and hence all oppression, the walls, the barriers, and the prisons, so that hearts become full of trust and all can enjoy the same freedom and the same dignity. Then we would ask that you make a particular effort to encourage your particular nation to stop the embargo imposed upon us and to restore its aid to the Palestinians. Many vital areas of community are in a desperate plight as a result of the withholding of this aid — not least justice, [the] economy, medical and educational [areas], etc.

As all Christians across the world celebrate Easter together, we wish everyone, at home and abroad, that joy which our Blessed Lord's Resurrection brings. We ask God to bestow upon all the joy and the power of the Resurrection so that the words of Jesus become real as He said: "I have come so that they may have life and have it to the full" (St. John 10:10).

Christ is Risen! He is risen indeed!

May you experience a Happy and Holy Easter!

Jerusalem, April 2007

Patriarchs and Heads of the Churches in Jerusalem

Patriarch Theophilos III of Jerusalem
Patriarch Michel Sabbah, R.C. Latin
Patriarch Torkom II Manooghian, Armenian Orthodox
Fr. Pierbattista Pizzaballa, O.F.M., Custos of the Holy Land
Archbishop Anba Abraham, Coptic Orthodox
Archbishop Swerios Malki Murad, Syrian Orthodox
Archbishop Abouna Matthias, Ethiopian Orthodox
Archbishop Paul Sayyah, Maronite
Bishop Suheil Dawani, Anglican
Bishop Munib Younan, Lutheran
Bishop Pierre Malki, Syrian Catholic
Bishop George Baker, Greek Catholic
Fr. Rafael Minassian, Armenian Catholic

A Message for International Church Action for Peace in Palestine and Israel, June 3rd-9th, 2007

As Patriarchs and Heads of Local Christian Churches in Jerusalem, we call upon our fellow Christians in this Land and across the world to join us in the **International Church Action for Peace in Palestine and Israel,** particularly during the period [of] **June 3rd to 9th 2007.**

This year marks the 40th Anniversary of Occupation[31] by the Israelis of land previously held by Palestinians. It is totally unacceptable for the situation to continue where the Palestinians endure daily hardships and humiliations with deprivations of International Human Rights, allegedly to ensure the safety and security of the Israelis, whereas we believe the security of Israel is dependent on the freedom and justice of the Palestinians.

Already we have declared our considered opinion for the future of Jerusalem (see Status of Jerusalem, November 2006), recognizing the right of the three Faiths — Jewish, Christian, and Moslem — and the needs of the two Peoples. Now we sincerely believe it is time to intensify action, particularly through negotiation, to end the Occupation, establish an independent Palestinian State — consistent with U.N. Resolutions 242 and 338[32] — and with borders clearly defined, thus giving both Peoples, Israelis and Palestinians alike, human dignity, security, and equal opportunities.

Many injustices have to be reversed, not least the restoration of land to lawful indigenous owners and the so-called Security Wall demolished.

For us as Christians, this Land is unique since God chose to reveal His love for human beings here when He gave His Son to be born in Bethlehem; to die on the Cross and on the third day to rise again here in Jerusalem. When Jesus revealed much of the Father's will to us in what we know as the Sermon on the Mount, he particularly declared: **"Blessed are the peacemakers, for they shall be called the sons of God."** *Matthew, ch. 5, v. 9*

All of us, together, must clearly affirm we are God's children and so give specific support to work diligently for peace now.

So, on behalf of our Churches, Communities, and Organizations in Palestine and Israel, we call on people of goodwill, across the world and not least those in Government, to join us in our efforts for peace especially during the period [of] **June 3rd to 9th 2007.** Naturally we ask our Christian sisters and brothers to make this period one of specific and diligent prayer for peace in this Holy Land.

The Prophet Micah shows us clearly the object and intention of all our efforts when he says: "**This is what the Lord asks of you: act justly, love mercy, and *walk humbly* with God.**" *Micah, ch. 6, v. 8*

Feast of Pentecost 2007

Patriarch Theophilos III of Jerusalem
Patriarch Michel Sabbah, R.C. Latin
Patriarch Torkom I Manooghian, Armenian Orthodox
Fr. Pierbattista Pizzaballa, O.F.M., Custos of the Holy Land
Archbishop Anba Abraham, Coptic Orthodox
Archbishop Swerios Malki Murad, Syrian Orthodox
Archbishop Abouna Matthias, Ethiopian Orthodox
Archbishop Paul Sayyah, Maronite
Bishop Suheil Dawani, Anglican
Bishop Mounib Younan, Lutheran
Bishop Pierre Malki, Syrian Catholic
Bishop George Baker, Greek Catholic
Fr. Rafael Minassian, Armenian Catholic

An Urgent Call from the Heads of Churches to the Members of Fateh and Hamas

On the recent 40th Anniversary of the Occupation we urged all sides to work for peace and the establishment of an independent Palestinian state. How painful and awful, then, that now we have to say stop all domestic fighting.

The fighting has struck at the most vulnerable timing, thus diverting International attention away from the National issue with its priorities and so disappointing the Palestinian people's hopes of attaining independence together with freedom from Occupation with its related aspects.

This domestic fighting where the brother draws his weapon in the face of his brother is detrimental to all the aspirations of achieving security and stability for the Palestinian people.

In the name of the One and only God as well as in the name of each devastated Palestinian, many of whom are still dying, we urge our brothers in Fateh and Hamas movements to listen to the voice of reason, truth, and wisdom. So we implore that you immediately announce the cessation of all bloody fighting and return back to the path of dialogue and attempt through understanding to solve all differences. In this urgent appeal we would draw attention to that which both parties have in common, assuring them that it is greater than their differences. The national and land cause must be greater than any other consideration.

In this belief we urgently ask both movements to listen and put aside all weapons, so concentrating on ending the Occupation in a peaceful manner based on National fundamentals and International legitimacy in order to achieve freedom for all the people together with an independent Palestinian state with Jerusalem as its Capital.

June 14th, 2007

ΦΡ

Christmas Message 2007

"He came to his own, and his own received Him not. But as many as received Him, to them gave He power to become the sons of God, even to them that believe on His name; which were born, not of blood, nor of the will of the flesh, nor of the will of man, but of God." St. John, ch. 1, vv. 11-13

Dear Sisters and Brothers,
Greetings.

Another Christmas is upon us and still we seek Peace for this Holy Land amidst continuing hardships. At the same time it is important for us to reflect carefully on what the Evangelist is trying to put before us about God's gift to us of Jesus, born in Bethlehem's manger, together with the clear response God asks of each one of us.

Amidst our difficulties, we need to meditate upon what links us in the same time to God and this land. In the Land, we ask for our freedom, for the end of the Occupation. We mention the difficulties coming from "the Wall of Separation" that has transformed our cities in[to] big prisons.

With God, we are linked because our dignity comes from His dignity, and we are His children and the work of His hands. And we must keep in mind that it is not fleshly descent or human effort which makes us the children of God, and it is not human strength alone that makes us strong. Rather, it is faith in our Lord Jesus Christ, the Eternal Word of God. Christmas reminds us that our faith is not only a human belonging to a group, or to a community different from the others by its religion. We are called to make a personal commitment to Jesus. Such a commitment tells the world and particularly those around us that we are prepared to witness and live by our reliance on Jesus the Word of God, born in Bethlehem, . . . who brought to us durable and firm peace in our hearts.

So often human beings believe they are capable of making peace through their own efforts, demanding conditions of their own choosing. However, when God gave us His Son to be born of a human mother and to experience all aspects of human life, He did so in order that we might discern the way to resolve our difficulties from His example and teaching. Therefore we pray for ourselves in order to understand the strength God gave us when He gave us His Eternal Word born in Bethlehem. So we pray for our political leaders, that God may inspire them and make them examine their conduct and demands in the light of God's commandments, always remembering their own accountability to Him, in this very life and in the process of the conflict itself.

So, dear Sisters and Brothers, whilst we are truly conscious of the many problems of unemployment, poverty, and frustration which many of you continue to face each day, we would still urge you to remember the words of the Apostle:

May "the peace of God rule in your hearts . . ." and "the word of Christ dwell in you richly in all wisdom." Colossians, ch. 3, vv. 15-16

We as Christians must continue to offer our prayers to God for all those around us who are struggling to care for their families, not least the young children and the elderly. We rejoice with those families now enjoying the company of those recently released from prison whilst persisting in our efforts to encourage the release of thousands more who have the same right to have back their freedom and return to the joy of their families and children.

Amidst our sufferings, we share the sufferings of the others. We have a particular thought for the countless thousands across the world who have endured great disasters as a result of the devastating cyclones and subsequent floods of recent months. We pray for them. And for all of us we repeat the verse of the Gospel:

"God so loved the world, that He gave His only begotten Son, that whosoever believeth in Him should not perish, but have everlasting life."
St. John, ch. 3, v. 16

To our Sisters and Brothers across the world: we are greatly encouraged by your continuing pilgrimages to this Land: we thank you for your presence with us. During your pilgrimage as well you learn at first hand the difficulties of your fellow Christians here as well as following in the footsteps of our Blessed Lord. Thank you for your prayers and the many expressions of your love and care for everyone here.

If Peace is to come to this Land, it needs even greater effort from all concerned — ordinary citizens as well as political leaders. Christmas reminds us that God gave us the Prince of Peace to be born in Bethlehem, so we must all seek that peace for everyone in this Holy Land, be they Palestinian or Israeli, Christian, Moslem, or Jew and Druze. He tells us that we are able to make peace and overcome all obstacles with the power which the Prince of Peace, born in Bethlehem, brought us.

We wish everyone a truly Happy Christmas and God's richest blessings on their homes and families.

Jerusalem, December 2007

Patriarch Theophilos III of Jerusalem
Patriarch Michel Sabbah, R.C. Latin
Patriarch Torkom I Manooghian, Armenian Orthodox
Fr. Pierbattista Pizzaballa, O.F.M., Custos of the Holy Land
Archbishop Anba Abraham, Coptic Orthodox
Archbishop Swerios Malki Murad, Syrian Orthodox
Archbishop Abouna Matthias, Ethiopian Orthodox
Archbishop Paul Sayyah, Maronite
Bishop Suheil Dawani, Anglican
Bishop Mounib Younan, Lutheran
Bishop Pierre Malki, Syrian Catholic
Bishop Baker, Greek Catholic
Fr. Rafael Minassian, Armenian Catholic

In the Name of God, End the Siege over Gaza

One and a half million people imprisoned without proper food or medicine. 800,000 without electricity supply. This is illegal collective punishment, an immoral act in violation of the basic human and natural laws as well as International Law. It cannot be tolerated anymore. The siege over Gaza should end now.[33]

Voices from our people there say, "We feel the threat of being exterminated by this siege."

In the Name of God, we, the Heads of Churches in Jerusalem and the Holy Land, urge the International Community, President Bush, and the leaders of Israel to put an end to this suffering and call upon Israel to activate Prime Minister Salam Fayyad's initiative for Palestinian responsibility [and] control of the borders, thus ensuring sufficient normal flow of medicine, food, fuel, and goods to Gaza.

We urge the International Community and the European Union to act according to their recent pleas. There is no time to waste when human life is endangered.

We urge the Palestinian Leadership to unite in ending their differences for the sake of their people in Gaza. Put the differences aside and deal with this crisis for the good of all human beings, demonstrating that you care for your brothers and sisters who have suffered enough already. We would say to all concerned parties: While ever you persist in firing rockets into Israel, you encourage public opinion outside this Land to feel there is a justification for this siege.

We urge Israel to act responsibly and to immediately end this inhuman siege. To deny children and civilians their necessary basic commodities [is] not the way to security but rather throws the region into further and more dangerous deteriorations. This siege will not guarantee the end to rocket firing, but will only increase the bitterness and suffering and invite more revenge, while the innocents keep dying. True peace-building is the only way to bring the desired security.

We pray for the day when the people of Gaza will be free from Occupation, from political differences, from violence, and from despair. We pray for the Israelis and Palestinians to respect human life and God's love for every human life, and [for] the human life and dignity of both people.

With the Prophet we keep praying and hoping:

The Jerusalem Heads of Churches Speak

> *"A bruised reed he will not break, and a smoldering wick he will*
> > *not snuff out.*
> > *In faithfulness he will bring forth justice;*
> *he will not falter or be discouraged till he establishes justice on earth.*
> > *In his law the lands will put their hope."*
>
> (Isaiah 42:3-4)

Heads of Churches in Jerusalem and the Holy Land

January 2008

A Call for Presence and Prayers

As I complete editorial work on this manuscript for publication, I read and re-read the most recent statement by the Jerusalem Heads of Churches, issued on 30 December 2008: "On the current devastating situation in Gaza."[1] It is a cry to Israelis and Palestinians, to the various Palestinian factions, and to the international community to "intervene immediately and actively stop the bloodshed and end all forms of confrontation." I join their cry, as I reflect on two strong and significant strands that run throughout the twenty years of statements by the Jerusalem Heads of Churches.

The first strand is precisely the persistent, and ever more urgent, appeal to the international community, particularly to the worldwide Christian community: stand in solidarity with Christian sisters and brothers in the Holy Land. The appeal is for prayer, for presence, and for pressure on governments and the United Nations. The appeal is for assistance and for advocacy.

This appeal arises, in some measure, from "an exasperation with the international community."[2] That is to say, the Jerusalem Heads of Churches, together with all Palestinians, cannot understand how the international community can ignore — year after year for sixty years — the violation of international laws and human rights conventions.[3] The appeal to the international community also arises from an affirmation: the city of Jerusalem is a city of universal significance. This affirmation is articulated most powerfully in the 14 November 1994 statement and, again, in the 29 September 2006 statement. Because of this unique character of Jerusalem, international collaboration and agreement are crucial for the city's future as a city holy to three religions. For this reason alone, the Jerusalem Heads of Churches appeal to the international community to implement international law, lest the architecture of occupation alter the status of the city irreparably.

Therefore, the appeal to the international community by the Jerusalem Heads of Churches arises also from a realistic reckoning of the situation. "Facts on the ground" are — day after day — being more fully established. The exclusionary wall. The expansion of settlements. The building of settler-only ring roads. The tramline to connect the outer ring of settlements to the city center of Jerusalem. Construction continues ceaselessly, making it ever more clear that the two parties — Israelis and Palestinians — cannot stop this remorseless unilateral activity, and end the occupation, by themselves. The relationship between Israelis and Palestinians is too asymmetrical as regards power. These are not well-matched parties able to sit together and come to an agreed-upon, balanced resolution of acrid and bitter conflict. Too much blood has been shed for too many years.

Nonetheless, a second refrain runs through the statements of the Jerusalem Heads of Churches: hope. Not an idea of hope. Hope born of acts of resistance and acts of solidarity. As has been noted above, the Jerusalem Heads of Churches themselves took action. They not only published statements. The Heads of Churches gathered to pray, and went to pray with their people. They led ecumenical prayer services and days for fasting. They joined boycotts, organized relief convoys, and marched in solidarity from Jerusalem to Bethlehem. They closed churches in protest, and rang bells on occasions of crisis and at times of celebration.

It is precisely because the Heads of Churches bore public witness to the words of their statements — word become flesh — through these twenty years that these statements, taken together, are a testament of hope. The hope that suffuses these statements is not "hope for" an outcome. Indeed, the more I have learned about and the longer I have lived amid the situation of Palestinian Christians, I have become convinced that these statements give an account of an unaccountable hope.

An account of an unaccountable hope. These statements, these texts in which the Jerusalem Heads of Churches speak of hope, can be understood only in Palestinian context. For the unaccountable hope of which account is given is hope that partakes of the Palestinian sense of *sumud* — steadfast-ness, refusing to submit, staying put, refusing to leave, resisting the ongoing injustice and oppression. Again and again (here in the 4 May 1992 statement), the Jerusalem Heads of Churches remind "our people": "We have been witness to the Lord in the birthplace of Christianity for the last two thousand years. We stand firm in our faith and determination to safeguard the Holy Places, and we will continue to do so for the ultimate glory of God, against all odds." Against all odds. An account of an unaccountable hope.

The hope of which account is given is also hope that proclaims the Gospel. The Christmas message of 1989 declares, "The message of 'peace on earth' which was proclaimed from the fields of Bethlehem brings consolation and a ray of hope to all the afflicted and suffering." And the Christmas message of 1996 echoes this emphasis:

> At this time of uncertain peace, the Christian community is called to nurture Christ's presence in this land. We must be the crib that embraces and protects the Prince of Peace, that represents the message of love and hope to the whole community and to all peoples. We must prepare Him room so that we might be His hands and feet, taking the initiative for peace.

The spirit of hope articulated in the statements is captured succinctly by the Easter messages of the Jerusalem Heads of Churches. In the 2007 Easter Message, for example, speaking about Paul's letter to the Christians in Philippi, the Heads of Churches make this proclamation:

> The statement he sets before the Philippians is regarded by many people as the most powerful: "All I want to know is Christ and the power of His Resurrection and to share His sufferings." In this short sentence he links the Cross and the Resurrection. The sufferings he has to face for his faith lead him to become conscious of the power of the Resurrection given to those who truly believe, through the power of the Holy Spirit. . . . In the midst of sufferings we reach the power of the Resurrection and the power of the Spirit that enable us to take away the oppressions that are imposed upon us.

The Jerusalem Heads of Churches are steadfast as an Easter people and call Palestinian Christians — "our people" — to be "the living stones" of the land called holy. They thereby encourage their people, a people who lives under occupation, suffering displacement, dispossession, hardship, and the humiliation of checkpoints. This occupation is enforced in violation of international law, which the international community is unable or unwilling to enforce or implement.

Finally, in these statements — taken to be a Jerusalem Testament — hope is found at the intersection of Cross and Resurrection. The Cross and the Resurrection. Each may be borne or borne witness to only in intimate relation to the other. This perhaps most profoundly points to a secure, just peace for the "two peoples and three religions" of this land called holy. A secure, just peace for Israelis is possible only with Palestinians. A secure, just peace for Palestinians is possible only with Israelis. Slowly, Israelis realize that they are at a crossroads: Do they choose to be a Jewish state or to be a single, secular state? Slowly, Palestinians realize they too are at a crossroads: Do they choose apartheid and accelerated colonization, or a single, secular state?

But now is a time so urgent. Israeli political leadership is in disarray, as is Palestinian political leadership. Extremists hold sway on all sides.

It was in a time so urgent — during the outbreak of the first Intifada — that the Jerusalem Heads of Churches came together and took unprecedented initiative in January 1988. This Jerusalem Testament — twenty years of their faithful, prophetic witness — gives account of an unaccountable hope: Palestinians and Israelis may together take an unprecedented initiative for a future of mutual flourishing. There can be life abundant for all. This is Gospel. May this Word become flesh.

MELANIE A. MAY
June 2009

Endnotes

Notes to the Introduction

1. Lisa Hajjar, in her study of the Israeli military court system in the occupied territories, identifies the linchpin of the Israeli occupation when she speaks of the reality of "the carceral nature of Israeli military rule in the West Bank and Gaza." She continues: "*Carceralism* is the term I use to describe Israeli rule over Palestinians in the West Bank and Gaza because it captures the fact that they are treated collectively as suspect and punishable and are imprisoned, literally in that thousands or tens of thousands are in prison at any given time, and equally literally in that, like prisoners, they are 'unfree.' The military court system is an institutional centerpiece of this carceralism, part of a broader array of governing institutions and practices in which Palestinians are enmeshed and tracked in grids of surveillance, subjected to restrictive codes of conduct and interaction, physically immobilized through the use of permits, closures, curfews, checkpoints, and walls, and incarcerated in huge numbers." See Lisa Hajjar, *Courting Conflict: The Israeli Military Court System in the West Bank and Gaza* (Berkeley and Los Angeles: University of California Press, 2005), p. 186.

2. D.-M. A. Jaeger spoke of "the inherent pluriformity of the Christian presence in the Holy Land," referring to "'devout men from every nation under heaven' (Acts 2:5), with their different rites, and at the time, distinct ecclesiastical structures" and so on. (See D.-M. A. Jaeger, "Christianity in the Holy Land: The Main Issues — An Introduction," in *Papers Read at the 1979 Tantur Conference on Christianity in the Holy Land,* ed. D.-M. A. Jaeger [Tantur, Jerusalem: Ecumenical Institute for Theological Research, 1981], p. 32.) At the same conference, Richard B. Rose noted, "Differences, then, existed in Palestine, as in Egypt and Syria, but here, in the Holy Land, the variety of opinions and traditions was kaleidoscopic." He then reflected, "While this inhibited unity, it also inhibited the division of the province into two or three clashing factions. . . . Within this framework of a greater diversity, all the laity and monks, priests and bishops of the country did share the country freely together — they shared the shrines, and shared a common monastic spirituality." (See Richard B. Rose, "The

Crusader Period in the Holy Land and Ecclesiology," in *Papers Read at the 1979 Tantur Conference on Christianity in the Holy Land,* p. 172.) These insights help ground historically the comment made by Father Frans Bouwen: "The fact that the Heads of Churches could come together in a time of conflict to make common statements reflects an ancient, deep-seated longing for unity" (personal conversation with the author, June 2008).

3. In 1950, the director of the Western Europe Division of the Israeli Foreign Ministry defined the prevailing view of the Christians in the Holy Land. He explained to Israel's minister in Rome, "*We are not dealing with relations with Christians but with relations with Arabs who happen to be Christians,* and regarding whom there are certain security considerations and stringent rules." By 1954, the advisor on Christian affairs to the Israeli minister of religious affairs reported, "Despite our concessions to the churches and the Christian communities in Israel, and despite the many benefits we have showered on them, we are now at loggerheads with almost all of them. Our relations with the Catholics are very bad, relations with the Protestants are deteriorating daily, and even the Orthodox, the Armenians, the Copts, and the Syrians have complaints and grievances which . . . are not voiced out loud because these communities have no patron at the moment who is willing to do battle for them." See Uri Bialer, *Cross on the Star of David: The Christian World in Israel's Foreign Policy, 1948-1967* (Bloomington and Indianapolis: Indiana University Press, 2008), pp. 125-26, 122.

4. While the act of issuing these statements was a political act by the Christian Heads of Churches living under Israeli occupation, the statements themselves are not political. That is to say, the statements do not take political positions or set forth a particular political program of action.

5. Christmas Message 1996. Hannah Arendt wrote, "The miracle that saves the world, the realm of human affairs, from its normal, 'natural' ruin is ultimately the fact of natality. . . . It is, in other words, the birth of new men and the new beginning, the action they are capable [of] can bestow upon human affairs faith and hope. . . . It is this faith in and hope for the world that found perhaps its most glorious and most succinct expression in the few words with which the Gospel announced their 'glad tidings': 'A child has been born to us.'" See Hannah Arendt, *The Human Condition,* 2d ed. (Chicago: University of Chicago Press, 1998), p. 247.

6. See www.btselem.org/Downloads/separation_barrier_map_eng.pdf. For a fuller discussion of the Wall, the construction of which began in June 2002, along with the Israeli rationale for building it, the route it follows, and the consequences of its construction, see *The Wall: Fragmenting the Palestinian Fabric of Jerusalem,* ed. Robert D. Brooks (Jerusalem: International Peace and Cooperation Center, 2007). See also *Against the Wall: Israel's Barrier to Peace,* ed. Michael Sorkin (New York, London: The New Press, 2005) and Eyal Weizman, *Hollow Land: Israel's Architecture of Occupation* (London and New York: Verso Press, 2007).

7. The policy and practice of house demolitions began during the British Mandate, when the British used it to "deter" Palestinian resistance or to enact collective punishment. After 1948, the Israelis demolished hundreds of houses in Palestinian villages inside what became the State of Israel. Today, according to Jeff Halper of the Israeli Committee Against House Demolitions, the purpose of house demolitions is "to confine the 3.7 million Palestinians of the Occupied Territories, together with the 1.3 million Palestinian citizens of Israel, to small, disconnected enclaves . . . on about 15 percent of the entire country. . . . It's

clear that the demolition policy is part and parcel of *nishul,* dispossession; turning the Land of Israel into an exclusively Jewish space — or at least a Jewish-controlled space; a sustained 60-year process of de-Arabization and Judaization." Halper estimates that approximately 18,000 Palestinian homes in the Occupied Territories have been demolished since 1967. He is clear: the demolitions are in violation of the Fourth Geneva Convention, Article 53, which states, "Any destruction by the Occupying Power of real or personal property belonging individually or collectively to private persons . . . is prohibited." He is also clear on the effects of the destruction: ". . . the demolition of a home is the demolition of a family." See Jeff Halper, *An Israeli in Palestine: Resisting Dispossession, Redeeming Israel* (London and Ann Arbor: Pluto Press, 2008), pp. 45-46, 55-56. For statistics, past and continually updated, see www.icahd.org; www.btselem.org.

Toine van Teeffelen, a Dutchman living with his Palestinian wife and their children in Bethlehem, concurs that the demolition of a house is more than the destruction of a building, noting that a "house" is not simply a building. A house is a "living stone," as conveyed in the Arabic word *Beit* (as in Bethlehem or Beit Sahour or Beit Jala). A Palestinian house, that is to say, is "a hospitable place, a life-giving symbol of fertility and fruitfulness. . . ." See Toine van Teeffelen, *Bethlehem Diary: Living Under Siege and Occupation, 2000-2002* (Bethlehem: Publication in the Culture and Palestine Series, 2002), p. 113.

8. In 1946, on the eve of the declaration of the State of Israel, there were 31,400 Palestinian Christians living in Jerusalem. According to the Israel Central Bureau of Statistics, in 2006, there were 10,000. The number is projected to drop to 5,300 in the next seven years, if Israeli policies continue — withdrawal of Jerusalemite identity cards; children not registered as Jerusalemites; limits on re-unification of spouses in cases where one has a Jerusalemite identity card and the other does not; etc. In addition, the number of Christians in the city is dropping because of economic depression due to the Wall, limited housing expansion licenses, tax burdens, and isolation from the West Bank. See "Jerusalem Christians — Residency Rights at Risk," prepared by Yusef Daher, Jerusalem Inter-Church Centre, St. Peter Street, Jaffa Gate, Old City, P.O. Box 741, Jerusalem 91000 (yusef66jrs@yahoo.com; Jcc@wcc-coe.org). Estimates are that, when the State of Israel was established, there were 400,000 Palestinian Christians in the Holy Land; today it is estimated there are 60,000. Abe Ata, an Australian-based Palestinian Christian, is quoted as saying, "The Palestinian Christian is an endangered species." See *Ecumenical News International,* no. 4 (23 April 2008): 21.

9. Samah Jabr, a psychiatrist practicing in her native Jerusalem and on the West Bank, writes, "In Jerusalem, Israel continues its subtle, continuous and systematic expulsion of Palestinians — a quiet *Nakba.* Via a system of paper, permits, proof, and permissions that determines who's in and who's out of the city, it is deliberately suffocating the natural growth of Palestinian families who have lived there for generations." See *Washington Report on Middle East Affairs* 27, no. 4 (May/June 2008): 33.

10. The central committee of the World Council of Churches, meeting in Geneva during 13-20 February 2008, issued a statement condemning attacks on civilians in the Gaza Strip and in Israel, and called member churches "to remind the government of Israel of the need to fulfill its international obligations as an occupying power, under the Geneva Conventions, to guarantee the provision of food, medicine, fuel, and water supplies and essential services, such as electricity and sanitation to the Gaza Strip." See http://www.oikoumene

.org/en/resources/documents/central-committee/geneva-2008/reports. For conditions in Gaza, see also "The Gaza Bombshell: Politics and Power," *Vanity Fair,* April 2008 (http://www.vanityfair.com/politics/features/2008/04/gaza200804). And also in April, Samah Jabr wrote, "What is happening in Gaza today is not a humanitarian crisis; rather it is another *Nakba,* another war. . . . The *Nakba* is not simply an historical event of the past. It is a deliberate program, a process of occupation, transfer, and genocide of the Palestinian people and their national identity to create an empty land to be populated by Jewish immigrants" (*Washington Report on Middle East Affairs* 27, no. 3 [April 2008]: 23).

Already in the mid-1990s, *Ha'aretz* reporter Amira Hass commented, "To me, Gaza embodies the entire saga of the Israeli-Palestinian conflict; it represents the central contradiction of the State of democracy for some, dispossession for others; it is our exposed nerve." See *Drinking the Sea at Gaza: Days and Nights in a Land under Siege,* trans. Elana Wesley and Maxine Kaufman Lacusta (New York: Henry Holt, 1996), p. 7. For a sustained analysis and reflection on the situation in Gaza, from a twenty-year perspective, see Sara Roy, *Failing Peace: Gaza and the Palestinian-Israeli Conflict* (London, Ann Arbor: Pluto Press, 2007).

11. For a comprehensive overview of Israeli settlements in the Occupied Territories, see www.btselem.org/Downloads/settlements_map_english.pdf. In July 2005, the International High Court of Justice ruled that Israeli settlements are in breach of the 4th Geneva Convention, which regulates the rights of occupied peoples, and which specifies that an occupier may not move inhabitants onto occupied land.

12. The Palestinians refer to the creation of the State of Israel in 1948 as their *Nakba* or catastrophe; Israel's occupation of the West Bank and Gaza in 1967 is said to be a *niksa* or defeat, setback. One reporter has commented, ". . . they have yet to coin a term for their present situation. It is, by any definition, a calamity. . . ." See *The Economist,* 23 February 2008, p. 62.

13. See *Remembering Deir Yassin: The Future of Israel and Palestine,* ed. Daniel McGowan and Marc H. Ellis (New York: Olive Branch Press, 1998) for accounts of the massacre and reflections on honest remembrance of Deir Yassin that may open a way toward solidarity in a land of conflict.

14. "Other peoples have suffered great tragedies, but the Palestinians' trauma not only refuses to reach closure, it has a horrible habit of repeating itself. Worse yet, its effects continue to poison politics within the wider region and beyond." See "The Wandering Palestinian," in *The Economist,* 10 May 2008, p. 57.

15. In 1929, H. C. Luke, Chief Secretary to the British Mandate Government of Palestine, commented, "It is probably true to say that no question more constantly exercised the Moslem rules of Palestine and took up more of their time than the ever recurring difficulties and disputes arising out of the circumstance that the Christian Holy Places in Jerusalem and Bethlehem were not in one ownership but were shared and served by several communities. In this respect the experience of the British Mandatory Government has not differed greatly from that of their Ottoman predecessor." See H. C. Luke, "Introductory Note," in L. G. A. Cust, *The Status Quo in the Holy Places* (Jerusalem: Ariel Publishing House, 1980). This book was originally published in 1929, after riots were precipitated in August 1929 over Jewish and Muslim rights to the Western Wall, and the Mandatory Government set up a special commission to clarify and maintain the Status Quo.

16. For a comprehensive narrative of Palestinian Christianity, see Donald E. Wagner, *Dying in the Land of Promise: Palestine and Palestinian Christianity from Pentecost to 2000* (London: Melisende, 2003). Two more readily accessible introductions to Jerusalem churches are Betty Jane Bailey and J. Martin Bailey, *Who Are the Christians in the Middle East?* (Grand Rapids: Wm. B. Eerdmans, 2003), esp. pp. 150-58, and Alison Hilliard and Betty Jane Bailey, *Living Stones Pilgrimage: With the Christians of the Holy Land* (London: Cassell, 1999).

17. In the earliest centuries, the Christian church was divided into three Patriarchates: Rome, Alexandria, and Antioch. Until 451 C.E., Jerusalem was a bishopric of Antioch. Another significant action taken by the Council of Chalcedon was the controversial extension of the authority of the bishop of Constantinople. The passage of Canon 28 effectively confirmed the bishop of Constantinople as equal in rank to the bishop of Rome.

18. See Bialer, *Cross on the Star of David,* pp. 179ff.

19. In the fourteenth and fifteenth centuries, another Orthodox church, the Georgian, was one of the most influential in the Holy Land. The church owned the Monastery of the Cross in Jerusalem, where it is said the true cross was made. It also owned the Monastery of St. James, Calvary, and the Monastery of St. Theodoros near Bethlehem, and held the keys to the Holy Sepulchre. Without adequate support from outside the Holy Land, by the middle of the seventeenth century the Georgians had lost most of their properties. See Saul P. Colbi, *A History of the Christian Presence in the Holy Land* (Lanham, Md., and London: University Press of America, 1988), pp. 73-74.

20. The Order of St. Francis was founded in Italy in the early years of the thirteenth century. Franciscans are also known as "minori" to indicate their poverty and humility.

21. See Sergio I. Minerbi, *The Vatican and Zionism: Conflict in the Holy Land, 1895-1925,* trans. Arnold Schwarz (Oxford: Oxford University Press, 1990), p. 6. See also Colbi, *A History of the Christian Presence in the Holy Land,* pp. 75ff.

22. Bernard Heyberger, "The Development of Catholicism in the Middle East (16th-19th Century)," in *Christianity: A History in the Middle East,* ed. Habib Badr (Beirut: Middle East Council of Churches, 2005), pp. 645-46. The rupture was institutionalized in the political authority in the nineteenth century, when the Supreme Porte officially recognized the Armenian Catholic Church in 1830. By 1848 all the Eastern Catholic churches had gained complete independence. Heyberger argues: "As a result, the distance between Catholics and Orthodox, as well as between Christians and Muslims, became much greater, and confessionalism, characterized by a strong authority of the clergy over the congregation, and a resolute determination to separate every confession from other neighboring confessions, was firmly established" (p. 646). This was further consolidated by nineteenth-century European intervention and led to the bitter interchurch conflicts later that century and into the twentieth century.

23. Wesley H. Brown, "Protestant-Catholic Relations in the Holy Land," in *Papers Read at the 1979 Tantur Conference on Christianity in the Holy Land,* p. 238. Brown goes on to say that the appeal reveals the attitude toward the ancient churches of Jerusalem, and he quotes: "It is well known that for ages various branches of the Christian Church have had their convents and their places of worship in Jerusalem. The Greek, the Roman Catholic, the Arme-

nian, each can find brethren to receive him, and a house of prayer in which to worship. . . . The pure Christianity of the Reformation alone appears as a stranger" (p. 238).

24. Because the Church of Prussia was non-episcopal, the new bishop would perforce be consecrated as an Anglican bishop; thus those filling the position would need to be Anglican by birth or by conversion. Nomination for the bishopric would be alternated between the British and Prussian rulers. See Colbi, *A History of the Christian Presence in the Holy Land*, p. 111.

25. During these years the so-called Restoration movement was gaining ground among evangelical Christians in England and elsewhere. The movement was dedicated to the return of Diaspora Jews to Palestine in order to rebuild Jerusalem. This would be a prelude to their conversion, which would then lead to the second coming of Christ.

26. The *Statement of Proceedings relating to the Establishment of the Bishopric*, in W. T. Gidney, *The History of the London Society for Promoting Christianity among the Jews: From 1809-1908* (London, 1908), p. 207. Cited by Brown, "Protestant-Catholic Relations in the Holy Land," p. 239.

27. Colbi suggests that among the reasons for this separation was the already mentioned stipulation that Lutheran ministers seek Anglican consecration as bishop. In addition, nearly fifty years after the initial agreement, when the King of Prussia became Emperor of a newly united Germany, a new prestige for the German Lutheran Church seemed in order. This new prestige was enacted in 1898 when Wilhelm II entered the Jaffa Gate of Jerusalem to dedicate the Church of the Redeemer and the Augusta Victoria Stiftung on Mount Scopus, named in honor of his wife, and including the Church of the Ascension. See Colbi, *A History of the Christian Presence in the Holy Land*, p. 116.

28. See Colbi, *A History of the Christian Presence in the Holy Land*, pp. 110-21.

29. In the later decades of the nineteenth century, some Palestinian nationalists were involved in the Arab nationalist movement based in Damascus. Others constituted "Palestine First," a group whose agenda was shaped in direct response to the perceived dangers of the British Mandate and Zionist immigration in Palestine. The goal of "Palestine First" was local political independence. See Muhammad Muslih, "The Rise of Local Nationalism in the Arab East," in *The Origins of Arab Nationalism*, ed. Rashid Khalidi, Lisa Anderson, Muhammad Muslih, and Reeva S. Simon (New York: Columbia University Press, 1990), pp. 167-85. See also Muhammad Muslih, *The Origins of Palestinian Nationalism* (New York: Columbia University Press, 1988), ch. 7, and Yehoshua, "The Political Awakening of the Palestinian Arabs and Their Leadership towards the End of the Ottoman Period," in *Studies on Palestine during the Ottoman Period*, ed. Moshe Ma'oz (Jerusalem: Magnes Press, 1975).

30. Ilan Pappe, *A History of Modern Palestine: One Land, Two Peoples*, 2d ed. (Cambridge, New York: Cambridge University Press, 2006), p. 47. The Palestine Native Church Council was formed in 1905, and was composed mostly of converts from either the Eastern Orthodox Churches or the Roman Catholic Church, this despite the clarity of the *Statement of Proceedings Relating to the Establishment of the Bishopric:* "He will establish and maintain . . . relations of Christian charity with other Churches represented in Jerusalem, and in particular with the Orthodox Greek Church; taking care to convince them that the Church of England does not wish to disturb, or divide, or interfere with them. . . ." See W. T. Gidney,

The History of the London Society for Promoting Christianity among the Jews, p. 207, cited by Brown in "Protestant-Catholic Relations in the Holy Land," p. 239.

31. Pappe, *A History of Modern Palestine,* p. 47.

32. By 1852, a decree of the Ottoman sultan, a *firman,* made the conversion of Ottoman subjects — i.e., Eastern Christians — legal. Already in 1847, having heard of "the existence of the Protestant menace," Pope Pius IX had issued the Apostolic Brief *Nulla celebrior* to restore the Latin Patriarchate as resident in Jerusalem, in part because of his worry about Protestant "proselytizing." (See Brown, "Protestant-Catholic Relations in the Holy Land," p. 241.) This Roman Catholic restoration, in turn, upset the Greek Catholic Church, whose Patriarchal Vicar bore titles of Jerusalem as well as Antioch and Alexandria. From the Greek Catholic Patriarchal point of view, therefore, a Latin Patriarch was redundant; this is a view that was still heard well into the twentieth century. Likewise, the Franciscan fathers were no less disconcerted by the re-establishment of the Latin Patriarchate; from their point of view, the Custos functioned as Bishop for the Holy Land. See Colbi, *A History of the Christian Presence in the Holy Land,* pp. 112, 121-22.

33. The Convent of Deir el-Sultan is adjacent to the Holy Sepulchre and consists of a courtyard and cluster of low buildings. Both the Coptic and the Ethiopian Orthodox Churches claim possession. The story of this ongoing dispute is a complicated part of the history of conflict over the Holy Places. See Cust, *The Status Quo in the Holy Places,* pp. 30ff. In an Ethiopian text, the *Kebra Negast,* the Queen of Sheba travels to Jerusalem to hear the wisdom of Solomon from his own lips. While there she conceives a son of his. During that night, Solomon dreams the sun "suddenly withdrew itself [away from Israel], and it flew away to the country of Ethiopia, and it shone there with exceeding great brightness for ever, for it willed to dwell there." Tradition also holds that the Ark of the Covenant resides in Ethiopia. Cited by Edward Fox in *Sacred Geography: A Tale of Murder and Archeology in the Holy Land* (New York: Henry Holt, 2001), p. 39.

34. It is said that "between 1630 and 1637, the right of pre-eminence in the sanctuaries alternated between the Greek Orthodox and the Roman Catholics no fewer than six times." See Colbi, *A History of the Christian Presence in the Holy Land,* p. 84.

35. L. G. A. Cust notes, ". . . during this period of international contention the smaller rites decline, if they do not drop out altogether, being unable to bear the exactions of the Turkish Government, which was intent on making the utmost out of the dissensions of the Christians" (*The Status Quo in the Holy Places,* p. 8).

36. The *firman* of 1852 was basically a confirmation of the *firman* of 1757. Very soon thereafter, the Crimean War began, a war that some argue was waged among rival Christian protectors of the Holy Places. The Status Quo was re-affirmed internationally in 1856 by the Treaty of Paris, and again in 1878 by the Treaty of Berlin, which concluded the war between Russia and Turkey. The Treaty of Berlin introduced the term *Status Quo* and declared that "no alterations can be made in the status quo in the Holy Places." See Walter Zander, *Israel and the Holy Places of Christendom* (London: Weidenfeld & Nicolson, 1971), p. 54. See also Walter Zander, "On the Settlement of Disputes about the Christian Holy Places," *Israel Law Review* 8, no. 3 (1973).

37. See Cust, *The Status Quo in the Holy Places,* p. 11.

38. After the uneasy armistice of 1948, the primary concern of Christian churches was

assurance that the Israeli government would honor the Status Quo agreements; the primary concern of the Israeli government was the Christian missionary work among Jews. In this regard, the focus of particular Israeli concern was Catholics and evangelical Protestants from the West. See Bialer, *Cross on the Star of David*, esp. pp. 93ff.

39. Ecumenical services of prayer for Christian unity began in the early 1960s. These were initiated by a small, informal group — the Ecumenical Circle of Friends — that still meets monthly in various Jerusalem locales. This Ecumenical Circle of Friends continues to coordinate the program of the annual Week of Prayer for Christian Unity, although the ecumenical services are planned by the churches directly, and are often led by the Heads of Churches themselves. See Frans Bouwen, "Celebration of the Week of Prayer for Christian Unity in Jerusalem," *The Ecumenical Review* 59, no. 4 (October 2007): 430-36.

40. In their Joint Communique, the Pope and the Patriarch say of their meeting, "Two pilgrims, their eyes fixed on Christ."

41. The Tantur Ecumenical Institute, inaugurated in September 1972, is built on land given in 1110 by the King of Jerusalem, Baldwin I, to the Knights of the Order of St. John. Having been lost after the defeat of the Latin Crusader Kingdom, it was obtained by the Austro-Hungarian Empire and the Knights of the Sovereign Order of Malta; the Knights of Malta built a hospice administered by the Brothers of St. John of God. When the Brothers left, the property devolved to the Salesian Fathers. See Colbi, *A History of the Christian Presence in the Holy Land*, pp. 314-15.

42. In his recent article, Frans Bouwen notes, "For various reasons the Greek Orthodox Church has until recently remained most hesitant in taking part in the Week of Prayer. Everybody regrets it deeply, because this church claims to be the most ancient in Jerusalem and has the greatest number of faithful in the country" ("Celebration of the Week of Prayer for Christian Unity in Jerusalem," p. 433).

43. Clearly, this hesitancy is not reflected by worldwide Orthodoxy, as indicated by the Jerusalem encounter of the Ecumenical Patriarch with Pope Paul VI in 1964.

44. Zander, *Israel and the Holy Places of Christendom*, p. 102.

45. Zander, *Israel and the Holy Places of Christendom*, pp. 105ff.

46. Since the founding of the State of Israel, there have been tensions regarding the guarantee of privileges and historic rights, freedom of access and worship, protection for the Holy Places, and so on. Early on, Israel forged bilateral agreements addressing issues specific to individual churches. For example, in relation to the Vatican, the Israelis were troubled by the Vatican's nonrecognition of the new state and its support for the U.N. proposal to internationalize the city of Jerusalem. In relation to the Protestants, as noted above, the primary concern was missionary activities. In relation to the Greek Orthodox Church, the preoccupation was to exploit the near bankruptcy of the church as an opportunity to buy or lease prime real estate. See Bialer, *Cross on the Star of David*, for fuller explication.

47. Here it is important to note differences in patterns of church-state relations between East and West. Eastern churches, particularly of the Byzantine tradition, have traditionally been wholly aligned with rulers of the state. Western churches, in contrast, have — whether in terms of "city of God" and "city of man" or in terms of two kingdoms and so on — distinguished themselves, in some measure, from civil authorities. Not surprisingly, then, anecdotal indicators suggest the strongest impetus for the joint public statements came

from the Latin Patriarch, together with the Anglican and Lutheran bishops. Here I owe a debt of gratitude to Professor Emerita Anna Marie Aagaard, University of Aarhus, for her insight into this church-state distinction, contributed at the Scholars' Colloquium I led at Tantur on 4 June 2008.

48. Until Sabbah's election in 1988, the post of the Latin Patriarch in Jerusalem was occupied by an Italian. This caused endless conflict between local Arab priests and European clergy.

49. The "children of stones" were young men and boys who had grown up in refugee camps in Gaza and on the West Bank. By the late 1980s, they were frustrated by what they perceived as their parents' quietism in the face of the post-1967 Israeli occupation. Choosing to resist the occupation, they picked up rocks and threw them at the occupying soldiers. Within weeks of the outbreak of the Intifada, a Syrian poet published a poem to "Atfal al-Kajarah," the "children bearing rocks." Thereafter, they were referred to as the "children of stones."

50. My gratitude to Ida A. Jones, Quality Translations. Period., in Binghamton, New York.

Notes to Chapter One

1. Article 49 of the 1949 Fourth Geneva Convention Relative to the Protection of Persons in Time of War, a cornerstone of international human rights law, states, "The Occupying Power shall not deport or transfer parts of its own civilian population into the territory it occupies" (quoted in Jeff Halper, *An Israeli in Palestine: Resisting Dispossession, Redeeming Israel* [London and Ann Arbor: Pluto Press, 2008], p. 252). The State of Israel ratified the Fourth Geneva Convention in 1951. The first settlement — Kfar Etzion — was begun in September 1967, a few months after the Six-Day War. Ten years later, Ariel Sharon laid his settlement map on the table and began to implement his strategy to change the map of the State of Israel. For a detailed narrative of Israel's settlements from 1967 to 2007, see Ideith Zertal and Akiva Eldar, *Lords of the Land: The War over Israel's Settlements in the Occupied Territories, 1967-2007,* translated from the Hebrew by Vivian Eden (New York: Nation Books, 2007). See also Gershom Gorenberg, *The Accidental Empire: Israel and the Birth of Settlements, 1967-1977* (New York: Henry Holt, 2006). For a discussion of the strategic definition of seven settlement blocs that confirm the incorporation of Judea and Samaria into Israel, and that undermine the establishment of a viable Palestinian state, see Jeff Halper, *An Israeli in Palestine,* pp. 165-68. Halper also notes that it is "supremely ironic" that "the foundations of modern human rights and internal humanitarian law . . . drew their inspiration and immediacy from the Jewish experience of the Holocaust," and that the first country called on "to honor the Geneva Conventions — unsuccessfully — was Israel." See Halper, *An Israeli in Palestine,* p. 117.

2. See Anton Shammas, "A Stone's Throw," *The New York Review of Books,* 31 March 1988; Catherine Cook, Adam Hanieh, and Adah Kay, *Stolen Youth: The Politics of Israel's Detention of Palestinian Children* (London: Pluto Press, 2003).

3. See, for example, Islah Abdul-Jawwad, "The Evolution of the Political Role of the

Palestinian Women's Movement in the Uprising," in *The Palestinians: New Directions,* ed. Michael Hudson (Washington, D.C.: Georgetown University, Center for Contemporary Arab Studies, 1990).

4. For a clear and concise account of these first two uprisings, relative to the first Intifada, see Baruch Kimmerling and Joel S. Migdal, *The Palestinian People: A History* (Cambridge: Harvard University Press, 2003), ch. 1, and also pp. 296ff.

5. David McDowell, *Palestine and Israel: The Uprising and Beyond* (London: I. B. Tauris & Co., Ltd., Publishers, 1989), p. 14. See also Kenneth Stein, "The Intifada and the Uprising of 1936-1939: A Comparison of the Palestinian Arab Communities," in *The Intifada: Its Impact on Israel, the Arab World, and the Superpowers,* ed. Robert O. Freedman (Miami: Florida International University Press, 1991). The most thoroughly researched history of the first Intifada is Mary Elizabeth King's *A Quiet Revolution: The First Palestinian Intifada and Nonviolent Resistance* (New York: Nation Books, 2007). Among the other now numerous descriptions and analyses of the Intifada are *Faith and the Intifada: Palestinian Christian Voices,* ed. Naim S. Ateek, Marc H. Ellis, and Rosemary Radford Ruether (Maryknoll, N.Y.: Orbis Books, 1992); *Justice and the Intifada: Palestinians and Israelis Speak Out,* ed. Kathy Bergen, David Neuhaus, and Ghassan Rubeiz (New York: Friendship Press, and Geneva: WCC Publications, 1991); Joost R. Hiltermann, *Behind the Intifada: Labor and the Women's Movements in the Occupied Territories* (Princeton: Princeton University Press, 1991); *Intifada: The Palestinian Uprising against Israeli Occupation,* ed. Zachary Lockman and Joel Beinin (Boston: South End Press, 1989); and Ze'ev Schiff and Ehud Ya'ari, *Intifada: The Palestinian Uprising — Israel's Third Front,* trans. Ina Friedman (New York: Simon & Schuster, 1990).

6. Avi Shlaim, *The Iron Wall: Israel and the Arab World* (London: Penguin Books, 2000), p. 489.

7. Sari Nusseibeh, quoted in King, *A Quiet Revolution,* p. 229. King also notes that the "roots of the popular committees date to 1936," during the Great Arab Revolt.

8. Mary Elizabeth King details the way in which the Intifada was carried on by local committees, radio broadcasts, and underground printing presses rather than by arms or even the throwing of stones. She names three nonviolent strategies implemented by Palestinians. First, they created local, populist committees that were the infrastructure of civil society. Second, the intellectual community articulated alternatives to armed revolt in ways that cultivated a sensibility for political compromise and negotiation. Finally, the Palestinians adopted techniques from nonviolent leaders and movements in other parts of the world — for example, from Gandhi in India and from anti-apartheid activity in South Africa.

9. Personal conversation at St. Anne's during the fall of 2007. St. Anne's Church is a twelfth-century Romanesque church located on the Via Dolorosa just inside St. Stephen's Gate, also known as the Lion's Gate because of the stone figures carved into its outside façade. Excavators believe that the site was first used for a pool that was cut in the eighth century B.C.E., a pool which fed the first Temple. The pool later was known as the Sheep Pool. During Roman times it was a healing pool where the sick, blind, and lame gathered to await a cure whenever the waters stirred. It is said to be the site where Jesus healed the crippled man (John 5:1-13). The original church was damaged by the Persians in 614. A restored church was destroyed in the eleventh century. The present church, built by Crusaders, was converted to a madrasa after Salah ad-Din Yusuf ibn Ayyub conquered the city in 1187. The

Ottoman Turks subsequently abandoned the structure, and it fell into ruin. Finally, in the late nineteenth century, the Ottomans offered the church to France. The French order of "White Fathers" — Missionaries of Our Lady of Africa — now administers the church.

10. For a detailed accounting of arrests, beatings, burnings, closures, and curfews, deaths by gunfire and in suspicious circumstances, of demolitions, expulsions, and injuries during the first year of the Intifada, see the publications of Law in the Service of Man (LSM, later renamed Al-Haq): *Punishing a Nation: Human Rights Violations during the Palestinian Uprising, December 1987–December 1988* (Al-Haq/Law in the Service of Man, 1988) and *Palestinian Victims of Torture Speak Out: Thirteen Accounts of Torture during Interrogation in Israeli Prisons* (Ramallah: Al-Haq, 1993). LSM or Al-Haq, founded by then-young Palestinian lawyers Jonathan Kuttab and Rajah Shedaheh, was the first Palestinian human rights organization and an affiliate of the International Commission of Jurists. See also Stanley Cohen and Daphna Golan, *The Interrogation of Palestinians during the Intifada: Ill-Treatment, "Moderate Physical Pressure," or Torture?* (Jerusalem: B'Tselem, 1991).

11. Charles M. Sennott, *The Body and the Blood: The Holy Land's Christians at the Turn of a New Millennium* (New York: Public Affairs, 2001), pp. 144-45.

12. The Franciscans became established as official representatives in Jerusalem of the Holy See, with the official title of Custodian of the Holy Land, in the twelfth century. In 1552 they were expelled by imperial decree from their headquarters in the Cenaculum on Mount Zion. They returned to the Custodianship in 1847, when the Latin Patriarchate in Jerusalem was restored.

13. The majority of Beit Sahour Christians are Greek Orthodox. Details of this journey of the Jerusalem Heads of Churches were gleaned from accounts by Patrick White in his *Children of Bethlehem* (London: Gracewing Books, 1991), pp. 135-40, and from personal conversations during the fall of 2007 with Father Frans Bouwen and Father Thomas F. Stransky, Rector Emeritus of the Tantur Ecumenical Institute. Mary Elizabeth King's account was also helpful. See *A Quiet Revolution*, pp. 232-33. Other accounts of the Beit Sahour tax revolt include M. J. Nojeim, "Planting Olive Trees: Palestinian Non-violent Resistance," Ph.D. dissertation, American University, 1993.

14. Hamas is a resistance group that emerged as an offshoot of the Egypt-based Muslim Brotherhood when the Brotherhood decided to join the Intifada in mid-December 1987. Part of an "Islamic bloc" of resistance groups, Hamas (Harakat-al-Muqawamah Al-Islamiyah), also known as the Islamic Resistance Movement, has sponsored kindergartens, clinics, youth centers, and schools, as well as armed operations. See Azzam Tamimi, *Hamas: Unwritten Chapters* (London: C. Hurst & Co., 2007).

15. D.-M. A. Jaeger notes that there had been "considerable apprehension regarding the intentions of the Jewish State" since 1948. He continues, ". . . consequently, there was also an unwillingness to risk provoking it, through 'over-insistence' on the exercise of inalienable rights and necessary freedoms, preeminently the right and freedom to evangelize, notwithstanding the avowal of democratic principles by the State." See D.-M. A. Jaeger, "Christianity in the Holy Land: The Main Issues — An Introduction," in *Papers Read at the 1979 Tantur Conference on Christianity in the Holy Land* (Tantur, Jerusalem: Ecumenical Institute for Theological Research, 1981), pp. 79-80.

16. Particularly since the nineteenth century, tensions among churches over custody of

the Holy Places ran high. Following the establishment of the State of Israel in 1948, churches had brokered bilateral relationships with the government. See Qustandi Shomali, "The Religious, Political, and Social Status of the Christian Communities in Palestine, c. 1800-1930," and Michael Dumper, "Church-State Relations in Jerusalem since 1948," in *The Christian Heritage in the Holy Land,* ed. Anthony O'Mahony, with Goran Gunner and Kevork Hintlian (London: Scorpion Cavendish Ltd., 1995). See also Uri Bialer, *Cross on the Star of David: The Christian World in Israel's Foreign Policy, 1948-1967* (Bloomington and Indianapolis: Indiana University Press, 2008), as well as Betty Jane Bailey and J. Martin Bailey, *Who Are the Christians in the Middle East?* (Grand Rapids: Wm. B. Eerdmans, 2003), esp. pp. 150-58, and Donald E. Wagner, *Dying in the Land of Promise: Palestine and Palestinian Christianity from Pentecost to 2000* (London: Melisende, 2003), pp. 129-212.

17. These included Fatah, the Popular Front for the Liberation of Palestine (PFLP), the Democratic Front for the Liberation of Palestine (DFLP), the Palestinian Communist Party, and the Islamists. See Kimmerling and Migdal, *The Palestinian People.*

18. For example, the 13 May 1988 *Communique no. 16* urged "the Masses of our People" to "the intensification of strikes against the police and collaborators . . . escalation of the refusal to pay taxes . . . boycott against Israeli goods . . . boycott against work in Zionist settlements. . . ." It further called upon lawyers to "reduce their fees" and "work towards exposing the inhuman conditions under which our people are living," and upon teachers to "participate . . . in the popular education effort." See David McDowell, *Palestine and Israel,* p. 5. The 22 January 1988 statement by the Jerusalem Heads of Churches includes similar directives: "dedicate next Friday, 29 January 1988, as a day for fasting and self-denial, . . . give what you thus save towards the support of our needy brothers and sisters," and so on. See also Shaul Mishal and Reuben Aharoni, *Speaking Stones: Communiques from the Intifada Underground* (Syracuse, N.Y.: Syracuse University Press, 1994).

19. Michael Dumper, *The Politics of Sacred Space: The Old City of Jerusalem in the Middle East Conflict* (Boulder, Colo., and London: Lynne Rienner Publishers, 2002), p. 122.

20. Personal conversation with the author in Jerusalem in the fall of 2007.

21. Dumper, *The Politics of Sacred Space,* p. 122.

22. Dumper, *The Politics of Sacred Space,* p. 125.

23. Nur Masalha, *The Bible and Zionism: Invented Traditions, Archaeology, and Post-Colonialism in Israel-Palestine* (London and New York: Zed Books, 2007), p. 175.

24. Dumper, *The Politics of Sacred Space,* p. 125.

25. Quoted by Dumper in *The Politics of Sacred Space,* p. 124.

26. Dumper, *The Politics of Sacred Space,* p. 124.

27. See most especially statements issued on 20 December 1990, 21 March 1991, and 4 May 1991. Here it is crucial to recall the law passed by the Knesset on 27 June 1967: "Protection of the Holy Places Law 1967." This law stipulates the following: "1. The Holy Places shall be protected from desecration and any other violation and from anything likely to violate the freedom of access of the members of the different religions to the places sacred to them or their feelings with regard to those places. 2.(a) Whoever desecrates or otherwise violates a Holy Place shall be liable to imprisonment for a term of seven years. (b) Any person who does anything likely to impair freedom of access to a Holy Place or to hurt the feelings of anyone to whom the place is sacred shall be liable to imprisonment for a term of five years."

See Walter Zander, *Israel and the Holy Places of Christendom* (London: Weidenfeld & Nicolson, 1971), p. 102. See also Saul P. Colbi, *A History of the Christian Presence in the Holy Land* (Lanham, Md., and London: University Press of America, 1988), pp. 201-2. Zander, referring to Holy Week celebrations in 1968, writes, "No serious incidents disturbed the celebrations. But some of those who had witnessed the Christian festivals in the preceding years commented on the sadness which now had overshadowed the events. . . . Many were uneasy or bewildered . . ." (p. 110).

28. Stephen Sizer, "The International Christian Embassy, Jerusalem: A Case Study in Political Christian Zionism," in *Speaking the Truth: Zionism, Israel, and Occupation,* ed. Michael Prior (Northhampton, Mass.: Olive Branch Press, 2005), p. 104.

29. Sizer, "The International Christian Embassy, Jerusalem," p. 105.

30. Sizer, "The International Christian Embassy, Jerusalem," p. 105.

31. Sizer, "The International Christian Embassy, Jerusalem," p. 104. For fuller discussions of the history, theology, archaeology, and politics of Christian Zionism, see also Stephen Sizer, *"Christian Zionism": Road-map to Armageddon?* (Leister, England: InterVarsity Press, 2004); *Challenging Christian Zionism: Theology, Politics, and the Israel-Palestine Conflict,* ed. Naim Ateek, Cedar Duaybis, and Maurine Tobin (London: Melisende, 2005); Victoria Clark, *Allies for Armageddon: The Rise of Christian Zionism* (New Haven and London: Yale University Press, 2007); Nur Masalha, *The Bible and Zionism;* Keith W. Whitelam, *The Invention of Ancient Israel: The Silencing of Palestinian History* (London and New York: Routledge, 1996); Dan Cohn-Sherbok, *The Politics of Apocalypse: The History and Influence of Christian Zionism* (Oxford: Oneworld Publications, 2006); Grace Halsell, *Prophecy and Politics: Militant Evangelists on the Road to Nuclear War* (Westport, Conn.: Lawrence Hill & Co., 1986); and Timothy P. Weber, *On the Road to Armageddon: How Evangelicals Became Israel's Best Friend* (Grand Rapids: Baker Academic, 2004).

32. This policy and procedure was already implemented shortly after the Six-Day War, in June 1967, when the Israeli government sent Yona Malachy of the Department of Religious Affairs to the United States to explore ways in which U.S. fundamentalism might become a strong ally of Israel. See Paul Boyer, *When Time Shall Be No More: Prophecy Belief in Modern American Culture* (Cambridge: Harvard University Press, 1992), p. 204. See also Weber, *On the Road to Armageddon,* and Yona Malachy, *American Fundamentalism and Israel: The Relation of Fundamentalist Churches to Zionism and the State of Israel* (Jerusalem: Hebrew University, 1978).

33. Sara Roy, *Failing Peace: Gaza and the Palestinian-Israeli Conflict* (London and Ann Arbor: Pluto Press, 2007), p. 42.

34. Recognizing "American double standards," Avi Shlaim nonetheless notes that U.S. support of the U.N. resolutions to condemn Israel for the Temple Mount Massacre, whether the United States was driven to this support or not, "demonstrated that there was a new equation in the making: an American approach to the Middle East based on an alliance with the Arabs and an Israeli approach to the Palestinians that largely ignored American, Arab, and international opinion." See Avi Shlaim, *The Iron Wall,* p. 476.

35. Avi Shlaim suggests that then-President George H. W. Bush, who "felt he owed no debt either to Israel or to American Jewry," forced Yitzhak Shamir to the table. He also suggests that two events enabled the United States to intervene and convene this conference to

negotiate a comprehensive peace settlement: "the defeat of the Soviet Union in the Cold War and the defeat of Arab radicalism in the Gulf War." See Shlaim, *The Iron Wall*, pp. 487, 485.

36. Shlaim, *The Iron Wall*, p. 487.

37. Here, for example, note the "Protection of Holy Places Law," passed by the Knesset in 1967, which states, "The Holy Places shall be protected from desecration and any other violation and from anything likely to violate the freedom of access of the members of the different religions to the places sacred to them or their feelings with regard to those places." See Zander, *Israel and the Holy Places of Christendom*, p. 102.

38. The small esplanade behind the Wailing or Western Wall in the Old City is sacred for Jews and Muslims. Jews refer to the area as Har Habayit or Temple Mount; Muslims call it Haram al-Sharif or Noble Sanctuary. It is the site of the Dome of the Rock, whence the Prophet departed on his night ride, and of the al-Aksa Mosque.

39. The so-called Temple Mount Massacre occurred on 8 October after Jewish extremists — the "Temple Mount Loyalists" — entered the courtyard area of the Haram al-Sharif to pray and thereby assert Jewish control of the area. Muslims who were there to worship threw stones. Israeli soldiers fired live ammunition. Twenty-one were killed; more than one hundred were wounded. Two U.N. resolutions condemned Israel. This was neither the first nor would it be the last time the Temple Mount or the Haram al-Sharif was the site of Jewish provocation of Muslims.

40. In August 1990, Saddam Hussein suggested that Iraq would consider withdrawing from Kuwait if Israel withdrew from all occupied territory and Syria from Lebanon. This proposal linked events, and the eventual war in the Gulf, with the Palestinian-Israeli conflict. Hussein became a savior figure for Palestinians. When war did break out, Israel refused to purchase gas masks for Palestinians and placed them under the strictest curfew.

Notes to Chapter Two

1. During this time, there were a number of noteworthy events: the Jerusalem closure in April 1993; the signing of the Oslo Accords in September 1993; and the Hebron Massacre in February 1994. These are discussed more fully in what follows.

2. Sara Roy, *Failing Peace: Gaza and the Palestinian-Israeli Conflict* (London and Ann Arbor: Pluto Press, 2007), p. 51. Article 49 of the Fourth Geneva Convention forbids deportations. See Jeff Halper, *An Israeli in Palestine: Resisting Dispossession, Redeeming Israel* (London and Ann Arbor: Pluto Press, 2008), p. 252.

3. "Israel-PLO Declaration of Principles on Interim Self-Government Arrangements," in *The Israel-Arab Reader: A Documentary History of the Middle East Conflict*, ed. Walter Laqueur and Barry Rubin, 5th rev. and updated ed. (New York: Penguin Books, 1969/1995), p. 601. There are numerous accounts of the Oslo Process. One of the clearest and most concise is by Ilan Pappe in *A History of Modern Palestine: One Land, Two Peoples*, 2d ed. (Cambridge: Cambridge University Press, 2004/2007), pp. 240ff. There are articulate critics of Oslo. Rashid Khalidi, for example, argues that Palestinian concessions were front-loads, while the issues requiring Israeli concession were reserved as Permanent Status Issues to be discussed later. See Rashid Khalidi, *The Iron Cage: The Story of the Palestinian Struggle for*

Statehood (Boston: Beacon Press, 2006), esp. pp. 158-64. One of the consequences of the back-loading of Israeli concession is what Ideith Zertal and Akiva Eldar call "silent annexation"; "the expanding of settlements for 'natural growth' could continue unhindered." See Zertal and Eldar, *Lords of the Land: The War over Israel's Settlements in the Occupied Territories, 1967-2007,* translated from the Hebrew by Vivian Eden (New York: Nation Books, 2007), p. 133. Another thing that has continued unhindered is the building of what Israeli architect Eyal Weizman calls the "structured chaos" of an intricate web of checkpoints, roadblocks, special security zones, closed military zones, and depth barriers, together with outposts and settlements, that ebbs and flows, and is able to "shrink and expand territory at will." This, then, is the spatial architecture of an occupation that is "an unregulated process of violent dispossession." Weizman also notes the tragic irony that, therefore, the Oslo Accords, which purportedly made Palestinians "sovereign *subjects*" in reality made them "*objects.* . . . It is precisely . . . in the Oslo years . . . that they have become most exposed to its [the occupation's] unrestrained power." See *Hollow Land: Israel's Architecture of Occupation* (London and New York: Verso Press, 2007), pp. 6, 5, 158. For other critiques of the Oslo Accords, see Edward W. Said, *The End of the Peace Process: Oslo and After* (New York: Pantheon Books, 2000), pp. xi-xxi, 312-21. See also Edward Said, *The Politics of Dispossession: The Struggle for Palestinian Self-Determination, 1969-1994* (New York: Pantheon Books, 1994).

4. As has been noted above, the Status Quo for the Christian Holy Places — in Jerusalem and Bethlehem, and on the Mount of Olives — was finalized in 1852, based on a 1757 agreement. Recently, there have been calls from Protestants to review the Status Quo because the contentiousness it has created is "embarrassing and scandalous to local Christians as well as vis-à-vis Muslims and Jews" (Naim Ateek, "The Future of Palestinian Christianity," in *The Forgotten Faithful: A Window into the Life and Witness of Christians in the Holy Land,* ed. Naim Ateek, Cedar Duaybis, and Maurice Tobin [Jerusalem: Sabeel Ecumenical Liberation Theology Center, 2007], p. 145). But the Greek Orthodox insisted that the Status Quo arrangements be specifically confirmed in the Heads of Churches' September 2006 statement on Jerusalem.

5. The concern of the Heads of Churches to confirm freedom of access for religious communities as well as individuals resounds declarations made by the U.N. Universal Declaration of Human Rights (Article 18) in 1948, by the Third Assembly of the World Council of Churches in New Delhi in 1961, and by the Vatican II document *Dignitatis Humanae,* issued in the mid-1960s.

6. To clarify: the Jerusalem Heads of Churches were not calling for the internationalization of the city. Nor did they look to the U.N. to guarantee a "special status" for Jerusalem. They were calling the international community to guarantee the city's universal character and access according to the international guarantee of access to the Suez Canal or Vatican City and the Danube. Cf. United Nations General Assembly Resolution 181: "The City of Jerusalem would be placed . . . under the International Trusteeship System by means of a Trusteeship Agreement, which would designate the United Nations as the Administering Authority" (*The Israel-Arab Reader,* p. 94). See also the U.N. Resolution on the Internationalization of Jerusalem (No. 303 [IV]), which again, two years later in 1949, declared "its intention that Jerusalem should be placed under a permanent international regime, which

should envisage appropriate guarantees for the protection of the Holy Places . . . and shall be administered by the United Nations" (*The Israel-Arab Reader,* pp. 115-16).

7. Article 39 of the Fourth Geneva Convention forbids the imposition of a permanent "closure" (Halper, *An Israeli in Palestine,* p. 252). Naomi Klein argues that this new policy was possible because, with the influx of Soviet refugees after the fall of the Soviet Union in the early 1990s, Palestinian labor was no longer needed. The implementation of the policy of "closure" transformed the Occupied Territories "from run-down dormitories housing the underclass of the Israeli state into suffocating prisons." See Naomi Klein, *Shock Doctrine: The Rise of Disaster Capitalism* (New York: Henry Holt & Co., 2007), p. 432.

Already the year after the 1967 war, a new urban master plan for Jerusalem was created. The stated purpose was its "unification." Central to this plan was the completion of a "security belt" to surround the eastern occupied areas of the city. Apartment complexes — Gilo, East Talpiot, French Hill, Ramat Eshkol, Ramot — displaced centuries-old Palestinian communities. Farther east, where the Mount of Zion begins its descent into the Jordan Valley, a huge settlement project — Ma'ale Adumim — became the cornerstone of a "unified" Jerusalem's "outer security belt." Other "outer security belt" settlements — effectively bedroom communities — include Giv'at Ze'ev, Efrat, and their spin-off outposts. There are at least two troubling consequences of these developments: (1) the physiognomy of the city has been more dramatically changed than at any other time in its many millennia of existence; and (2) Jerusalem is now constituted by ethnically homogeneous, and separated, sections. See Meron Benvenisti, *City of Stone: The Hidden History of Jerusalem* (Berkeley and Los Angeles: University of California Press, 1996), pp. 202ff., and Michael C. Hudson, "The Transformation of Jerusalem," in *Jerusalem in History,* ed. K. J. Asali, with an introduction by Rashid Khalidi (New York: Olive Branch Press, 2000), pp. 249ff. Moreover, comments Eyal Weizman, this "'Greater Jerusalem' became thus a sprawling metropolis reaching the outskirts of Ramallah in the north, Bethlehem in the south, and Jericho in the east — a massive section of the middle of the West Bank — isolating Palestinians from their cultural centres in Jerusalem and cutting off the north of the West Bank from the south. . . . Israeli activist Jeff Halper was therefore exaggerating when he stated that 'metropolitan Jerusalem *is* the occupation.'" See Weizman, *Hollow Land,* p. 26.

8. On 24 January 2007, Amira Hass wrote in the Israeli daily paper *Ha'aretz,* "Each of the many dozens of checkpoints has developed its own methods of harassment over the years. They derive from the implicit order behind the existence of every checkpoint: prevent Palestinian freedom of movement for the sake of the welfare of the Jewish settlements; that is to say — Israel. . . . Because the Palestinians have no alternative but to continue to pass through them, those checkpoints will continue to be representative of Israeli society." Hass is said to be one of a very few Israeli journalists who still roam around the Occupied Territories. She lives in Ramallah.

9. In order to retain their Jerusalem residency, Palestinians bear an ongoing burden of proof that their "center of life" is Jerusalem. It is estimated that, since 1967, approximately 6,000 Jerusalem identity cards have been confiscated. See B'tselem, *The Quiet Deportation: Revocation of Residency of East Jerusalem Palestinians* (Jerusalem: B'tselem, 1997), and B'tselem, *The Quiet Deportation Continues* (Jerusalem: B'tselem, 1998); see also www .btselem.org. In 1974, an amendment to a 1952 Israeli law made it possible for the Israeli gov-

ernment to revoke "the residency of Palestinians who resided outside Israel for seven years or who acquired citizenship or residency in another country" (Samith K. Farsoun and Naseer H. Aruri, *Palestine and the Palestinians: A Social and Historical History,* 2d ed. [Boulder, Colo.: Westview Press, 2006], pp. 331ff.). It is worth noting that many Israeli citizens, however, hold dual citizenship, most in the United States.

10. Article 27 of the Fourth Geneva Convention states, "Protected persons are entitled, in all circumstances, to respect for their persons, their honor, their family rights, their religious convictions and practices, and their manner and customs" (Halper, *An Israeli in Palestine,* p. 251).

11. The bedrock of the Oslo Accords was that neither the Israelis nor the Palestinians would take steps that would change the status of the Occupied Territories in ways that foreclosed negotiations on Permanent Status Issues. The closure of Jerusalem, which actually predated the signing of the Accords, land expropriation, and the building of settlements at an escalated pace — activities that characterized the years from 1992 to 1996 — indisputably compromised this bedrock. Moreover, increasingly violent means of enforcement of Israeli power were used: arrests, detention, house demolition.

12. Zertal and Eldar, *Lords of the Land,* pp. 147-48.

13. Hamas came into existence with the outbreak of the first Intifada in December 1987. On the evening of 9 December, the seven men who constituted the senior leadership of Al-Ikhwan Al-Muslimun (the Muslim Brotherhood) held an emergency meeting. These seven made the decision to transform the Ikhwan movement in Palestine into a resistance movement: Harakat Al-Muqawamah Al-Islamiyah (the Islamic Resistance Movement, or Hamas). Dr. Abd Al-Aziz Al-Rantisi drafted the first communiqué, which was released to the press on 14 December 1987. Al-Rantisi, along with two others of this group of seven — Sala Shihada and Sheik Ahmad Yassin — were assassinated by the Israelis in 2002 and 2004. Article 32 of the Fourth Geneva Convention forbids assassinations. See Halper, *An Israeli in Palestine,* p. 252.

Preparations for this moment had intensified during the previous ten years, as conditions in the Gaza Strip became more and more unbearable after the right-wing Likud party, led by Menachem Begin, came to power on 17 May 1977. Nearly thirty years earlier, on the morning of 9 April 1948, Menachem Begin was the leader of the Irgun commandos, who, together with the Stern Gang, attacked the Palestinian village of Deir Yassin. Over one hundred men, women, and children were systematically murdered.

Hamas published its charter in the summer of 1988. In April 1994, Hamas launched a series of suicide-bomb attacks to retaliate for the massacre at the al-Ibrahimi Mosque in Hebron and to express its frustration with the futility of the Oslo Accords. For an authoritative account of Hamas — its origins in 1987 to the present, its ideology, and a discussion of the strategy of suicide bombing — see Azzam Tamimi, *Hamas: Unwritten Chapters* (London: Hurst & Co., 2007), esp. chapters 1, 3, 7, and 8.

14. Halper summarizes the Oslo II agreement: it "carved the Occupied Territories into a complex mosaic of 'areas': 'A' drawn tightly around the major Palestinian population centers and, on paper, placed under Palestinian Authority (PA) control; 'B' giving the PA civil control over additional concentrations of villages but leaving security under effective Israeli control; and 'C' the 60 percent or so which contained the Israeli settlements, infrastructure,

and military facilities, under total Israeli control. . . . The idea was that over a series of phased withdrawals, 'C' would become increasingly taken over by 'B,' 'B' would steadily become 'A,' until . . . the Palestinians would have all the territory except the settlements, infrastructure, and military facilities. . . . The problem is that Israel hardly withdrew at all . . ." (*An Israeli in Palestine*, pp. 51-52).

15. *The Israeli-Palestinian Agreement on the West Bank and the Gaza Strip* (Oslo II), Chapter 5, Article 31 (7).

16. Al-Haram al-Sharif (the Noble Sanctuary) is to Jews the Temple Mount. It is an esplanade raised above deep valleys, upon which sat the first and second temples. Since the seventh century C.E. the site has been for Muslims the third holiest site on earth, upon which the Dome of the Rock and the al-Aqsa Mosque stand.

17. See Karen Armstrong, "The Holiness of Jerusalem," in *The Open Veins of Jerusalem*, ed. Munir Akash, 2d ed. (Syracuse: A Jusoor Book, 2005), p. 61.

18. On 14 October 2007, it was reported in *Ha'aretz* that the Israel Antiquities Authority was "set to renew its excavations in the coming days at the Mugrabi Gate near the Western Wall in Jerusalem, which may exacerbate tensions with neighboring countries ahead of next month's planned Annapolis peace summit." On 17 December 2007 the headline on the front page of *Ha'aretz* was "Cabinet Okays Renewing Controversial Mugrabi Excavation near Western Wall."

19. The Oslo Accords had promised that "a redeployment of Israeli military forces in the West Bank and the Gaza Strip will take place" (Article XII:1). See *The Israel-Arab Reader*, p. 604.

20. Mary Elizabeth King interviewed a former Israeli Defense Force officer who said that "Israel's first use of tanks in any Palestinian turbulence would not occur until September 1996 in Jerusalem, after Israel opened a tunnel in Jerusalem that runs alongside the Temple Mount and Haram al-Sharif, and street demonstrations in protest were followed by altercations." Reuven Gal, quoted in King, *A Quiet Revolution: The First Palestinian Intifada and Nonviolent Resistance* (New York: Nation Books, 2007), p. 360, n. 10.

21. Jabal Abu Ghneim, a hill adjacent to the traditional site of the Shepherds' Fields, was the site of a number of fifth- and sixth-century Byzantine monastic ruins.

Rev. Alex Awad, Dean of Students at Bethlehem Bible College and pastor of the East Jerusalem Baptist Church, recalls, ". . . the Israeli government in 1991 approved the confiscation of the land. . . . Palestinians objected and the international community condemned the move. Both Israeli and Palestinian peace groups demonstrated peacefully . . . but the Israeli government dismissed all of this opposition and proceeded with its plans. The first step in construction was the clearing of thousands of beautiful green trees, a unique feature of the hill. Palestinian anger finally boiled over. . . . In retaliation, the Israelis fired . . . with live bullets. . . . Although Palestinians eventually ceased their protests . . . their anger did not vanish. It is just such regularly recurring incidents that create fertile ground for terrorism." See Alex Awad, *Palestinian Memories: The Story of a Palestinian Mother and Her People* (Jerusalem: Bethlehem Bible College, 2008), p. 294.

22. Naseer H. Aruri, "Misrepresenting Jerusalem," in *The Open Veins of Jerusalem*, pp. 135-36. The Etzion bloc of settlement was the first to be established after the 1967 war. His Eminence Msgr. Lutfi Laham, Greek Catholic Patriarchal Vicar, declared, ". . . the new settle-

ment at Jabal Abu Ghneim . . . in reality is planned as a town to supersede Bethlehem, to suffocate Bethlehem economically and to cut it off physically from Jerusalem. . . . Is it still possible to speak honestly of a 'peace process' when one side, the more powerful, acts against peace deliberately, massively, and systematically as long-term policy? . . . To date the accomplishments of 'peace' amount to some legal contracts and accords. But without trust and respect among human beings these documents cannot bring peace. *Perhaps they are not meant to.*" See the *Bulletin of the Associated Church Press,* no. 396 (April 1997): 4.

In September 1967, just before the Jewish New Year, a small group initiated "the next phase of redemption, the Jewish settlement of the Greater Land of Israel. . . . The Etzion Bloc was selected as the bridgehead from the basically secular and pragmatic State of Israel, the boundaries of which had been demarcated by the end of the 1948 war, to the national religious Land of Israel, the boundaries of which had been extended by the battles of the 1967 war" (Zertal and Eldar, *Lords of the Land,* p. 5). Kiryat Arba was the lodestone of the Etzion bloc. Its proximity to Hebron became, in the words of Zertal and Eldar, "a hothouse of the entire settlement project, with its subversion and defiance of the law and of Israeli democracy; some who in their official capacity had been involved from the beginning admitted that the move had been a tragedy of error and that the government had been dragged after the settlers' lies and tricks. 'Kiryat Arba was a tragedy,' said Shlomo Gazit, the first coordinator of the activities of the territories, fifteen years later" (Zertal and Eldar, *Lords of the Land,* p. 24).

23. Aruri, "Misrepresenting Jerusalem," p. 136. See also Zertal and Eldar, *Lords of the Land,* pp. 245ff.

24. The drafting of this statement was begun in *The Open Veins of Jerusalem* following the signing of the Oslo Accords, in September 1993, during a time most people still hoped the peace process would be fruitful. This hope began to wane as final-status negotiations — on Jerusalem, refugees, settlements, borders, and sovereignty — that were to have commenced early in 1996 were postponed, and as subsequent agreements made it clear that, while the Palestinian Authority would administer Palestinian civilian life, Israel would retain security, border control, water rights, and most of the land. As Edward W. Said commented, "Far from ending, the Israeli occupation was simply repacked, and what emerged in the West Bank was about seven discontinuous Palestinian islands amounting to 3 percent of the land surrounded and punctuated by Israeli-controlled territory" (Said, *The End of the Peace Process,* p. xv). Marwan Bishara commented, "The Clinton team ignored the central issues of contention where solutions could bring stability, in favor of security relations, security preoccupations, and security measures. In Palestine itself, the 'security logic' of the peace process and America's exigency in underlining the logic of force had already been transformed into an authoritative 'logic of force' in the Palestinian entity" (Marwan Bishara, *Palestine/Israel: Peace or Apartheid — Occupation, Terrorism, and the Future* [London and New York: Zed Books; South Africa: Spearhead; Halifax: Fernwood Publishing, 2002/2004], p. 90). The preoccupation with security — in tandem with the "logic of force" based on the asymmetry of power between Palestinians and Israelis, occupied and occupier — turned "the peace process" into nothing more than a cover for Israeli expropriation of more land to build more settlements and settler-only roads.

25. This reference is to a well-known treatise or "Peregrinatio" that narrates the journey

of a devout woman to Egypt, the Holy Land, Constantinople, and so-called Asia Minor ca. 381-384. Egeria is thought to have been an abbess or a nun, possibly from Iberia, who had an impressive intellect and keen powers of observation. Her descriptions of sites of biblical events are related to liturgical practices, especially in Jerusalem and environs. See H. Sivan, "Who was Egeria? Pilgrimage and Piety in the Age of Gratian," *Harvard Theological Review* 81 (1988): 59-72.

26. Cyril was Bishop of Jerusalem from about 349. His most significant surviving work is a series of catechetical instructions delivered to candidates for Baptism on Holy Saturday. This series includes much material for reconstructing the Palestinian liturgy of the fourth century. See P. W. L. Walker, *Holy City, Holy Places: Christian Attitudes to Jerusalem and the Holy Land in the Fourth Century* (Oxford: Clarendon, 1990), esp. pp. 31-34, 116-30, 311-46.

27. See note 4 above. In a personal conversation in the fall of 2007, Father Thomas F. Stransky told me that this paragraph that calls for confirmation of the Status Quo agreements was added to a second draft at the request of the Greek Orthodox Church.

28. See note 6 above.

29. Marwan Bishara puts it well: ". . . Jerusalem should be the engine for peace, a force of stability and coexistence rather than a by-product of the peace process or, worse, a source of division and conflict" (*Palestine/Israel: Peace or Apartheid*, pp. 112-13).

30. These places were closed by Israeli military authorities in 1967 for "security reasons." A few years earlier, the Jordan had once again become accessible, but only on official pilgrimage dates, the last Thursday of October for the Latin Church and the eve of the Epiphany (18 January) for the Orthodox Churches. It is unknown whether the Jerusalem Heads of Churches received a reply to this letter.

31. At the same meeting where the Jerusalem Heads of Churches approved this message, they also stated their concern about the new land expropriations south of Jerusalem, in the Jabal Abu Ghneim area and within the territories of Bethlehem and Beit Sahour, for the purpose of building a new Jewish settlement to complete the encirclement of the Palestinian part of Jerusalem. In earlier times, this area was the location of numerous Christian monasteries. Now it will close the so-called Jerusalem Envelope of Jewish settlements.

32. This is probably a reference to the signing of what is often referred to as Oslo II — the September 1995 agreement that granted rule over all Palestinian cities (except Hebron) to the Palestinian Authority (Area A, about 4 percent of the West Bank) and joint Israeli-Palestinian rule over village areas (Area B). Expansive areas in the Jordan Valley as well as Jewish settlements and their access roads were to continue under Israeli rule (Area C). The phrase possibly also reflects the ethos in the months following the assassination of Prime Minister Rabin in November 1995.

33. Here the concern of the Heads of Churches, noted relative to the 6 April 1995 statement, became explicit. See note 31 above.

34. The events of which the Jerusalem Heads of Churches speak are the riots that followed the opening of the archaeological tunnel under the area of Al-Aqsa (the Temple Mount). These riots broke out across the West Bank and Gaza. Approximately 40 Palestinians and 11 Israelis were killed; more than 100 were wounded on each side. See pp. 49-50 above.

Notes to Chapter Three

1. As noted above, the 1993 closure of Jerusalem involved a new stringency regarding residency status for the population of Jerusalem.

2. *Proche-Orient Chrétien* (2000): 357.

3. Fatah is a Palestinian resistance movement founded by Yasser Arafat in the late 1950s. Fatah gained control of the Palestinian Liberation Organization (PLO) in 1969. Already training military cadres in the 1950s, Fatah was, at that time, the only organization to advocate armed struggle against Israel, first from its base in Jordan, then in Lebanon, and finally in Tunis. After the signing of the Oslo Peace Accords in 1993, Arafat and other Fatah members returned home and established headquarters in Ramallah, West Bank.

4. "Black March," say Ideith Zertal and Akiva Eldar, "was a turning point in the building of the barrier," or the Wall, as described by Palestinians. See Zertal and Eldar, *Lords of the Land: The War over Israel's Settlements in the Occupied Territories, 1967-2007*, translated from the Hebrew by Vivian Eden (New York: Nation Books, 2007), p. 420. Some sections of the Wall are metal fence, hedged by surveillance roads; in "Greater Jerusalem" the Wall is a massive thirty-foot-tall concrete barrier. See *The Wall: Fragmenting the Palestinian Fabric in Jerusalem,* ed. Robert D. Brooks (Jerusalem: A Publication of the International Peace and Co-operation Center, 2007).

5. Charles Enderlin, *The Lost Years: Radical Islam, Intifada, and Wars in the Middle East 2001-2006,* trans. Suzanne Verderber (New York: Other Press, 2007), p. 137.

6. According to Charles Enderlin, the IDF had begun preparations for an invasion and siege of Palestinian towns already in July 2001, with the code name "Different Field." When the operation was launched in March 2002, it was renamed "Defensive Shield," for the purpose of protecting "Israeli citizens from terrorism" (Enderlin, *The Lost Years,* p. 141).

7. See Raja Shehadeh, *When the Bulbul Stopped Singing: A Diary of Ramallah under Siege* (London: Profile Books, Ltd., 2003). Amira Hass gave this report from Ramallah: "On the evening of Wednesday, May 1, when the siege on Arafat's headquarters was lifted and the armored vehicles and tanks had rumbled out, the executives and officials of the [Palestinian Ministry of Culture] who had rushed to the site did not expect to find the building the way they had left it. But what awaited them was beyond all their fears, and also shocked representatives and cultural attachés of foreign consulates. . . . In other offices, all the high-tech and electronic equipment had been wrecked or had vanished. . . . In every room . . . books, disks, pamphlets, and documents were piled up, soiled with urine and excrement . . ." (*Ha'aretz,* 6 May 2002). Operation Defensive Shield, concluded Hass, was not to destroy "terrorist infra-structure," as stated by the IDF, but to destroy Palestinian civil infrastructure — for example, data banks "of the non-governmental organizations and research institutes devoted to developing a modern health system, modern agricultural, environmental protection, and water conservations. These are the data banks of human rights organizations, banks and private commercial enterprises, infirmaries, and supermarkets" (*Ha'aretz,* 6 May 2002). For the accounts of discharged soldiers who are veterans of the second Intifada, many of whom were in Ramallah at the time of the siege, see *Breaking the Silence: Testimonial Booklet #1.* For further information and testimonies in English, go to www.breakingthesilence.org.il. In her most recent novel, Sahar Khalifeh chronicles the 2002 siege of Ramallah, focusing on the

siege of Arafat's official headquarters in that West Bank city. See *The End of Spring,* trans. Paula Haydar (Northhampton, Mass.: Interlink Publishing Group, 2008).

8. See Mitri Raheb, *Bethlehem Besieged: Stories of Hope in Times of Trouble* (Minneapolis: Augsburg Fortress Press, 2004). For a journalistic perspective, see Joshua Hammer, *A Season in Bethlehem: Unholy War in a Sacred Place* (New York: Free Press, 2003). Eyal Weizman reports that Shimon Naveh "described how in this period 'the military started thinking like criminals . . . like serial killers. . . . They got allocated an area and researched it. . . . When they enter the area they know where to look . . . and they start killing. . . .'" See *Hollow Land: Israel's Architecture of Occupation* (London and New York: Verso Press, 2007), p. 197.

9. Mustafa Barghouti, speaking on the BBC about the violent behaviors of the Israeli soldiers toward medical personnel and international observers, said, "Where is the international community, human rights and international law? This is a dark day for Israel, for the West, for the world" (cited by Shehadeh in *When the Bulbul Stopped Singing,* p. 45).

10. In order to retain their Jerusalem residency, Palestinians must prove to the Ministry of the Interior that their "center of life" is Jerusalem. Jeff Halper clarifies: "Moving to affordable housing just beyond the municipal border invalidates that status, allowing the Interior Ministry to revoke the residency of those 'emigrants.'" See Halper, *An Israeli in Palestine: Resisting Dispossession, Redeeming Israel* (London and Ann Arbor: Pluto Press, 2008), p. 48.

11. This message was sent by the three Patriarchs to Yasser Arafat and Ehud Barak in advance of the Camp David summit during July 2000.

12. See not only the nineteenth-century Status Quo provisions, but also United Nations General Assembly Resolution 181: "In so far as Holy Places are concerned, the liberty of access, visit, and transit shall be guaranteed, in conformity with existing rights, to all residents and citizens . . . of the City of Jerusalem, as well as to aliens, without distinction as to nationality, subject to requirements of national security, public order, and decorum" (*The Israel-Arab Reader: A Documentary History of the Middle East Conflict,* ed. Walter Laqueur and Barry Rubin, 5th rev. and updated ed. [New York: Penguin Books, 1969/1995], p. 101). The last phrase, of course, invited wide-ranging and contentious interpretation and practice even before the resolution's passage on 29 November 1947.

13. See, for example, United Nations General Assembly Resolution on the Internationalization of Jerusalem, 1949 (Resolution No. 303[IV], in *The Israel-Arab Reader,* ed. Laqueur and Rubin, pp. 115-16.

14. Published in *The Jerusalem Times,* 6 October 2000.

15. The second Intifada, the Al-Aqsa Intifada, began the day after Sharon's provocative visit to Al-Haram al-Sharif on 28 September 2000.

16. This message was a specific response to a recent series of events. Early on the morning of 17 October, Rehavam Zeevi, who had just resigned as Minister of Tourism, was assassinated in a hotel in West Jerusalem. A cycle of violence began again. The IDF planted explosives that killed three cousins. Seeking revenge, militants from the Al-Aqsa Martyrs' Brigade fired from Beit Jala onto nearby Gilo. On the night of 18 October, the IDF re-occupied Beit Jala and neighboring Bethlehem, as well as five other West Bank towns, including Ramallah. By 20 October, the Palestinian death toll had reached eight. See Enderlin, *The Lost Years,* pp. 105ff.

17. *The Israel-Arab Reader,* ed. Laqueur and Rubin, pp. 91ff.

18. Lutheran Bishop Munib Younan also contacted the prime ministers of Norway and Sweden. These prime ministers in turn called Israeli prime minister Ariel Sharon. It was this intervention that abated the violence to some extent, at least in Bethlehem. See Raheb, *Bethlehem Besieged,* p. 24.

19. President Bush responded to Sharon at a press conference the next day: "Withdraw! Withdraw your troops immediately." But, as Victoria Clark reports, Jerry Falwell, sensing that Bush was becoming "a little anti-Israel," blasted the White House with 100,000 e-mails. There was no further call for withdrawal. Sharon's invasion continued. See Victoria Clark, *Allies for Armageddon: The Rise of Christian Zionism* (New Haven and London: Yale University Press, 2007), p. 217.

20. Clearly this is an excerpt of the appeal. As in the previous year, the Jerusalem Heads of Churches appealed for a fortnight of ecumenical prayers for peace, to take place from 15 August to 28 August, the dates of the Feast of the Assumption, according to the Gregorian calendar, and the Dormition of the Virgin Mary, according to the Julian calendar.

21. In a letter (which I was unable to find) that was made public on 11 October 2002, the Heads of Churches in Jerusalem expressed their profound concern about and questioned President George W. Bush's signing of HR 1646 (U.S. Congress) into law. This law contains a passage ratifying the proposed relocation of the U.S. Embassy to Jerusalem. The Heads of Churches demanded respect for international law concerning Jerusalem and warned the president that such an initiative risked compromising future peace efforts.

Notes to Chapter Four

1. On 9 July 2004, the International Court of Justice made the following declaration: ". . . all States are under an obligation not to recognize the illegal situation resulting from the construction of the wall in the Occupied Palestinian Territory, including in and around East Jerusalem. . . . It is also for all States, while respecting the United Nations Charter and international law, to see to it that any impediment, resulting from the construction of the wall, to the exercise by the Palestinian people of its right to self-determination is brought to an end" (quoted in Jeff Halper, *An Israeli in Palestine: Resisting Dispossession, Redeeming Israel* [London and Ann Arbor: Pluto Press, 2008], p. 244). The court's vote was 14-1, the lone dissenting vote being cast by the American judge. The United Nations General Assembly voted to accept the advisory opinion of the International Court of Justice decision: "1. The wall is being built on occupied territory and is therefore a violation of international law. 2. The wall construction should cease and it and the legal, administrative, and military regime that supports it should be dismantled. 3. Reparations should be paid to those who have suffered damages." This decision is quoted in *The Wall: Fragmenting the Palestinian Fabric in Jerusalem,* ed. Robert D. Brooks (Jerusalem: A Publication of the International Peace and Cooperation Center, 2007), p. 6. To read the 56-page opinion of the International Court of Justice, see http://www.bitterlemons.org/docs/ungawall.pdf.

2. For a stunning account of the Wall within "the logic of the late occupation," see Eyal

Weizman, *Hollow Land: Israel's Architecture of Occupation* (London and New York: Verso Press, 2007), esp. chs. 5 and 6, including p. 292 n. 3 and p. 309 n. 15.

3. In June 2000, just before the Camp David talks and despite all his claims of generosity, Ehud Barak had a fully articulated "separation" plan prepared. By June 2002, following Operation Defensive Shield, Barak's successor, Ariel Sharon, implemented the plan. Construction of a concrete-and-steel wall the length of the West Bank began. For an insightful discussion of Sharon's vision of separation, see Jonathan Cook, *Disappearing Palestine: Israel's Experiments in Human Despair* (London and New York: Zed Books, 2008), pp. 104ff.

After the occupation of the West Bank of the Jordan River, the Gaza Strip, and East Jerusalem in 1967, the Israeli government began strategic planning for demographic as well as territorial dominance, thereby assuring the state as a "Jewish state." The debate was between two strategies: "transfer" or "separation." Vladimir Jabotinsky was an early twentieth-century proponent of the latter. The "transfer" strategy for the sake of "an exclusively Jewish state," argues Israeli historian Ilan Pappe, was also an integral part of planning already in the 1920s. See Pappe, *The Ethnic Cleansing of Palestine* (Oxford: One World, 2006). See also Walid Khalidi, *All That Remains: The Palestinian Villages Occupied and Depopulated by Israel in 1948* (Washington: Institute for Palestine Studies, 1992), and Nur Masalha, *Expulsion of the Palestinians: The Concept of 'Transfer' in Zionist Political Thought, 1882-1948* (Washington: Institute for Palestine Studies, 1992).

4. Jonathan Kuttab, "The Ministry of Reconciliation," in *The Forgotten Faithful: A Window into the Life and Witness of Christians in the Holy Land*, ed. Naim Ateek, Cedar Duaybis, and Maurine Tobin (Jerusalem: Sabeel Ecumenical Liberation Theology Center, 2007), p. 171.

5. According to Jeff Halper, "While Palestinian residents of 'East' Jerusalem are confined to highly circumscribed enclaves, 35 percent of their land has been expropriated for Israeli settlements, roads, and other Israeli facilities since 1967, while the rest of their unbuilt-upon land, a full 54 percent of East Jerusalem, has been designated as 'open green space.' Palestinians may own their land but are denied the right to build upon it" (Halper, *An Israeli in Palestine*, p. 47). This post-1967 reality is based on the plan set forward by then Jerusalem mayor Teddie Kollek, a plan based on three principles: "expropriation of Arab-owned land, development of large Jewish neighborhoods in East Jerusalem, and limitations on development in Arab neighborhoods" (Amir S. Cheshin, Bill Hutman, and Avi Melamed, *Separate and Unequal: The Inside Story of Israeli Rule in East Jerusalem* [Cambridge: Harvard University Press, 1999], p. 37). Halper notes that the "overall goal" is known in Israel as the "Quiet Transfer," either confining Palestinians to ever-smaller enclaves or removing them altogether from the city (Halper, *An Israeli in Palestine*, p. 47). The language of "quiet transfer" was also employed by the Israeli human rights group B'tselem to talk about the consequence of massive house demolitions during the first four years of the first Intifada: the mass emigration of middle-class Palestinian families (Halper, *An Israeli in Palestine*, p. 193).

6. See Ideith Zertal and Akiva Eldar, *Lords of the Land: The War over Israel's Settlements in the Occupied Territories, 1967-2007*, trans. from the Hebrew by Vivian Eden (New York: Nation Books, 2007), esp. pp. 396ff.

7. President George Bush, after "arm-twisting" by the "Quartet" — the U.S., the European Union, Russia, and the U.N. — announced the Road Map in March 2003. It calls ex-

plicitly for the end of the Israeli occupation and for a "viable," independent, democratic Palestinian state. "Still," says Jeff Halper, "everyone knew that the Road Map was a dead letter even before it was issued. . . . The goal . . . would remain the same: an expanded Israel over a dependent and truncated Palestinian mini-state" (Halper, *An Israeli in Palestine,* p. 195).

8. This is my translation from the French.

9. Already in his 1996 Christmas message, Patriarch Michel Sabbah spoke about the system of permits restricting Palestinian freedom of movement and declared, "Every Palestinian town is . . . transformed by this system of permit into a LARGE PRISON" (*Bulletin of the Associated Christian Press* [February 1997]: 394).

10. This is my translation from the French.

11. In the fall of 2007, Vivi Siniora, the Danish-Palestinian artist long associated with the Tantur Ecumenical Institute, told me, anecdotally, that Yasser Arafat was forbidden to come to the celebration at the Church of the Nativity, Manger Square, Bethlehem, in 2003. Palestinian Christians who gathered there draped a kaffiyeh over his empty chair on the speaker's platform.

12. *Bulletin of the Associated Church Press,* no. 442 (September-October 2005): 19.

13. Two months before the election, Sharon suffered a massive stroke. His Vice-Premier, Ehud Olmert, was instead elected to succeed Sharon as Premier. In May, Olmert presented his "Convergence Plan" to a joint session of the U.S. Congress. Jeff Halper describes the plan as follows: "In it a Greater Jerusalem and the settlements — in which 80 percent of Israel's settlers live and into which the rest will be 'converged' — are annexed to Israel and a Palestinian state is sandwiched between Israel's *two* eastern borders: its 'demographic border' delineating the settlement blocs from the Palestinian areas, and its 'security border' along the Jordan Valley" (Halper, *An Israeli in Palestine,* p. 203). Faced with the fact that this plan was a unilateral plan, thereby contradicting the Road Map, Olmert hastily clarified that this "convergence" was more precisely a "realignment" of Israeli borders in an "interim" manner that conformed to the Road Map: "The Palestinians get their state, albeit a 'transitional' state with 'provisional borders.' And that's where we stay forever" (Halper, *An Israeli in Palestine,* p. 203).

14. These decisions, first and foremost, have to do with settlements and with the Wall and checkpoints. See Zertal and Eldar, *Lords of the Land.*

15. My translation is from the French.

16. David Rose, "The Gaza Bombshell," *Vanity Fair,* 9 March 2008. See also www.vanityfair.com/politics/features/2008/04/gaza200404.

17. Arafat died in November 2004, and Abbas, the new Fatah leader, was elected president in January 2005. Elections for the Palestinian Legislative Council were scheduled for July 2005, but were later postponed by Abbas until January 2006. Hamas won 56 percent of the seats in the Palestinian Legislative Council. When the Quartet — the U.S., the European Union, Russia, and the U.N. — demanded the new Hamas government renounce violence, recognize Israel's right to exist, and accept terms of previous peace agreements, Hamas refused. International aid stopped.

18. Raja Shehadeh, *When the Bulbul Stopped Singing: A Diary of Ramallah under Siege* (London: Profile Books Ltd., 2003), p. 7. Shehadeh goes on to say: "There was no insistence on a settlement freeze which the Delegation in Washington has made a condition for enter-

ing into any agreement with Israel. . . . As the negotiations were proceeding for a final agreement more settlements were being built and existing ones expanded at a faster pace than ever. . . . It took several years before people were able to grasp the disaster that was the Oslo Accords. When they did, the second Intifada broke out" (p. 142).

19. See, for example, Easter 1991, 14 November 1994, Christmas 2001, 7 July 2006, 22 August 2006, and, most poignantly, 3 April 2002 and 22 January 2008. This most recent appeal was a call for support in the face of the siege of Gaza, beginning 18 January 2008.

Shortly thereafter, Neve Gordon, who teaches in the Department of Politics and Government at Ben Gurion University in Beer-Sheva, Israel, wrote, "The experiment in famine began on Jan. 18. Israel hermetically closed all of Gaza's borders, preventing even food, medicine, and fuel from entering the Strip." Gordon continues, commenting that, while Defense Minister Ehud Barak's rationale — ongoing bombardment of Israelis across the border — seems logical, it conveniently ignores the fact that since the January 2006 democratic elections, Hamas has proposed several cease-fire agreements and has agreed to stop missile attacks in exchange for Israel ending its incursions into Gaza, the assassinations of political leaders, and the economic boycott. What is really at stake, says Gordon, is not missile attacks but "showing [Palestinians] who is in control, . . . breaking their backs, so that they lower their expectations and bow down to Israeli demands" (*National Catholic Reporter,* 8 February 2008, pp. 20, 24).

Also in February 2008, the World Council of Churches Central Committee, meeting in Geneva, Switzerland, from 13 to 20 February 2008, issued this statement: ". . . we express our deep sadness at the humanitarian situation in Gaza, increasing alarm at the incessant violations of human rights and ongoing losses of life among Palestinians and Israelis, and grave concerns at the future of the peace process for both Israel and Palestine. A chorus of international concern is calling for an end to the blockade of Gaza and reminding the government of Israel that collective punishment is prohibited by the Geneva Convention that governs its conduct in Gaza. We join our voices to these calls for mercy and justice, again. We do so today and for as long as the suffering continues, believing that a future for all can and will be found." See http://www.oikoumene.org/en/resources/documents/central-committee/geneva-2008/reports.

20. "By 1993," writes Matt Rees, "when its budget was at $50 million, Hamas was considering joining the political process as an Islamist party. Israeli agents saw the advantages of a group that would divert support from Arafat and secretly aided Hamas. With Israeli consent, the number of mosques in Gaza rose to more than 200. In 1967, under Egyptian rule, there were seventy-seven" (Matt Rees, *Cain's Field: Faith, Fratricide, and Fear in the Middle East* [New York: Free Press, 2004], pp. 34-35). After Arafat signed the Oslo Accords, Hamas and Fatah played a strategic game for the hearts and minds of Palestinians.

21. See Sylvain Cypel, *Walled: Israeli Society at an Impasse* (New York: Other Press, 2006). This volume was originally published as *Les Emmurés: La société israeliénne dans l'impasse* in 2005. Cypel argues that, first and foremost, it is the Israelis themselves who are walled in by a mind-set traceable to the beginnings of Zionism and the early Jewish national movement, a mind-set that ignores rather than engages "the other."

22. The Wall now fully encloses Bethlehem; Palestinians who want to travel to Jerusalem or elsewhere in the West Bank must have a permit and go through a checkpoint.

23. Yasser Arafat, said to be the father of Palestinian nationalism, founder of Fatah, and leader of the PLO and the Palestinian Authority, died on 11 November 2004.

24. Since the previous statement by the Jerusalem Heads of Churches, suicide bombings and IDF raids had escalated: 31 August, 15 September, 29 September, and so on. In October alone, 140 Palestinians and four Israelis were killed.

25. In February, one Israeli and twenty-nine Palestinians were killed, either during attacks or military operations in the West Bank and the Gaza Strip.

26. Jeff Halper articulates the view of most Palestinians: "The present historical moment finds us in Palestine/Israel at a fateful crossroads. From the point of view of Israel's political leadership, Israel has won its century-old conflict with the Palestinians. Surveying the landscape — physical and political alike — they can feel a great deal of satisfaction. Begin's charge to Sharon in 1977 has been fulfilled. The settlement project . . . ensures the permanent Israeli control over the entire Land of Israel. . . . The 'facts on the ground' are in place. . . . And the Separation Barrier constitutes Israel's expanded border. All that remains is the political act that transforms the Occupation into a permanent political reality. . . . The status quo only serves the de facto: Israel's control will only grow and deepen. . . . For Israel, the status quo is just as good as a peace agreement — maybe better, since Israel need make no concessions at all" (*An Israeli in Palestine,* pp. 207-8).

27. The international boycott began after the election of Hamas in the January 2006 elections. Commenting on these elections, Jeff Halper says, "The election of Hamas did not have to do only with issues of Fatah weakness and corruption. . . . It was an act, above all, of non-cooperation, perhaps the most powerful means of non-violent resistance the oppressed have when all other avenues have been closed. It is to the international community and, yes, Israel and Fatah as well, that the Palestinians carried their message: 'To hell with all of you!'" (*An Israeli in Palestine,* p. 209).

28. It is far from easy for churches in the U.S. to "break silence" and take actions toward justice. In an article that appeared in *The Christian Century,* 11 March 2008, it was reported, "The 7.9-million-member United Methodist Church is poised to become the next U.S. denomination to consider divesting from companies said to support Israeli military-security goals, a topic so controversial that it prompted the Presbyterian Church (U.S.A.) to redefine its own divestment program two years ago. At its quadrennial General Conference this April in Forth Worth, Texas, the Methodists will debate whether to pull church holdings in Caterpillar, which provides the Israel Defense Forces with bulldozers." These bulldozers are primarily used for house demolitions.

The article goes on to note, "The United Church of Christ, the Evangelical Lutheran Church in America, and the Episcopal Church have all stalled or reversed course on earlier attempts at divestment."

29. The Israelis refer to this war as the Second Lebanese War.

30. This is the first mention of the Druzes, a close-knit community living mainly in South Lebanon, Southwest Syria, and the Hawran district of Israel/northern Palestine. The Druzes' religion derived from Isma'iliya, an aggregation of Muslim groups, known for esoteric teachings that seem to have absorbed Persian gnosticism. Accordingly, the Druze community is divided into the initiates and the uninitiated or ignorant. While they believe in the

unity of God, they also believe in successive manifestations of the deity in human form, the last of which was Khalifa al-Hakim, who disappeared in 1021 C.E.

31. On the morning of Monday, June 5, the 1967 War, or Six-Day War, began. By the end, the Israeli army had occupied the territories on the west bank of the Jordan River (the West Bank), which had been under Jordanian rule; the Gaza Strip, which had been under Egyptian rule; and the Golan Heights, which had been part of Syria. Most significantly, the Israelis "unified" Jerusalem. For a thorough historical account of the lead-up to the war and a day-by-day account of it, see Tom Segev, *1967: Israel, the War, and the Year that Transformed the Middle East,* trans. Jessica Cohen (New York: Henry Holt & Co., 2005).

32. The U.N. Security Council Resolution 242 of 22 November 1967 addressed "the inadmissibility of the acquisition of territory by war and the need to work for a just and lasting peace in which every State in the area can live in security." U.N. Security Council Resolution 338 of 22 October 1973 "calls upon the parties concerned to start immediately after the cease-fire the implementation of Security Council resolution 242 (1967) . . . aimed at establishing a just and durable peace in the Middle East." See Appendix III in Alex Awad, *Palestinian Memories: The Story of a Palestinian Mother and Her People* (Jerusalem: Bethlehem Bible College, 2008), pp. 338-39.

33. Neve Gordon, in his 8 February 2008 article in the *National Catholic Reporter,* says this about the siege that began on January 18, 2008: "Power cuts . . . were extended to 12 hours per day. . . . At least 40 percent of Gazans have not had access to running water, which is channeled through electric pumps, and the sewage system has broken down. . . . Hospitals have been forced to rely on emergency generators, leading them to cut back, yet again, on the already limited services offered to the Palestinian population. The World Food Programme has reported critical shortages of goods and declared that it is unable to provide 10,000 of the poorest Gazans with three of the five foodstuffs they normally receive" (p. 20). For a twenty-year perspective, see Sara Roy, *Failing Peace: Gaza and the Palestinian-Israeli Conflict* (London and Ann Arbor: Pluto Press, 2007).

Notes to the Afterword

1. Available at http://www.lpj.org/newsite2006/news/2008/12/gaza-message-en-headschrches2008.html.

2. Toine van Teeffelen, *Bethlehem Diary: Living under Siege and Occupation, 2000-2002* (Bethlehem: Publication in the Culture and Palestine Series, 2002), p. 254.

3. Throughout the above chapters, violations of the Fourth Geneva Convention and other international legal rulings have been noted. Israeli violations of international law apparently have the backing of the United States. On 30 April 2008, Dennis Ross, former Clinton administration "peace process" point person, declared, "The issue, ultimately, is not one of international law. . . . You don't settle historic conflicts by having an approach that is based only on international law." See *The Washington Report on Middle East Affairs* 27, no. 5 (July 2008): 60.

Index

Index